My Pal Splendid Man

Will Jacobs and Gerard Jones

 Atomic Drop Press

ISBN 978-0-9965259-1-6
Published by Atomic Drop Press
www.atomicdroppress.com

Once again we dedicate this to our wives:

to Jennie Kajiko for lending her name

and

to Agnes Jacobs for contributing a splendid suggestion.

Contents

Introduction

It was 1982 and we had just sold our first book. After years of separately writing serious novels that no one wanted anything to do with, we had decided to try writing something together just for fun, and we surprised ourselves by conceiving, completing, and actually selling a humor book, *The Beaver Papers*. It would be over a year before the book actually hit the bookstores, and during that time, fired with enthusiasm to work together, we dreamed up one humor idea after another. Some of those ideas later saw print in the *National Lampoon*, one of them eventually became the comic book *The Trouble with Girls*, but the one we loved best and did the most work on is the one you are about to read.

We both lived in San Francisco, but not in the artistically edgy North Beach or Mission District that you read about in literary histories. We lived in the Richmond District, the foggy northwest corner of the city, a neighborhood of small apartment buildings with an almost suburban quality compared to the city that lay a bus ride away. We did most of the work at Will's place, a second-floor apartment at the corner of 42nd Avenue and Balboa Street, and so it came to serve as the actual setting for much of the book. The second-hand furniture, the less-than-stellar housekeeping, and the air of slightly charming shabbiness all left their imprint on the stories.

We didn't have much money then, and in our memories we seem to have subsisted almost entirely on rice and chili—the rice we cooked at home, the chili we bought at a takeout Mexican joint down the street. When we felt like splurging we'd drive down to Mr. Hot Dog's Cowboy BBQ, a Korean-owned diner on Geary Boulevard where a man could get full for less than four dollars. Our external lives weren't much, but our internal lives were rich—

if a bit peculiar. Besides surfeiting ourselves on William Faulkner, John Steinbeck, Ernest Hemingway, and other literary heavyweights, we also indulged in a shared obsession with the comic books of the 1960s. In our novels we tried to emulate the former, but we could never shake the temptation to do something creative with the latter.

And so were born the stories that would become *My Pal Splendid Man*. It started with a quickly scribbled scene which would eventually become the opening to the second story in this collection, in which a superhero drops in on his young writer friend Will Jones—not as a prelude to exotic adventures but to talk about life, books, and highballs. That scene grew into a story, and suddenly we were seized. For a few months our favorite thing to do was to get together, eat our chili, and spin out a new Splendid Man story. We did wind up sending our heroes off on exotic adventures, but they were adventures of the sort that grew out of the peculiar chemistry of their friendship.

Finally *The Beaver Papers* came out and made a modest splash. It earned us an invitation to write for the *National Lampoon* and the acceptance of our second book, a serious indulgence in our obsession called *The Comic Book Heroes*. By then we had begun to conceive *My Pal Splendid Man* as a book, but as life swept us along, we never found the time to finish it. After a while it became one of those projects in our drawers, remembered with great fondness but never returned to.

Thirty years later we opened that drawer. We read the stories again, first with nostalgia but then with the joy of rediscovery. Not only were they still alive to us but they reignited the fire that had filled us decades before. We found ourselves writing five new Splendid Man stories to round out the narrative and weaving new threads through all the episodes to hold them together as a book.

We were momentarily tempted to update the book's milieu, but then we thought better of it. Not only was Will's life built around the realities of being a would-be writer in the pre-internet age, not only were there some story elements that could really only work in the social context of the early '80s, but the essence of Splendid

Man himself was clearly inspired by things we were observing in comics at the time. The wholesome superheroes of the "Silver Age" were then being supplanted by a newer, darker sort of superhero; the tension of that moment was much of what went into defining our hero's character. So, despite the great temptation to fill Splendid Man and Will's world with iPads, hybrid cars, and kale, we've set the stories in the time they were originally conceived.

Fly with us, then, back through the time barrier to 1982. Ronald Reagan is in the White House. A dark grittiness is creeping into popular culture. The poor can still afford rent in parts of San Francisco. A writer needs White Out to correct a mistake. Will Jones strikes up a beautiful friendship with a fellow known as Splendid Man. And up and away we go.

We want to thank all the folks at Atomic Drop Press for giving us the opportunity to share these stories at last.

Will Jacobs and Gerard Jones
September 2015

Episode One
Splendid Man's Literary Discoveries

I opened the window, moved aside, and vibrated the teeth of my SOS Comb. Splendid Man zoomed into my apartment before I could count to one.

"What's the trouble, Will?" he said.

"I lost my damn keys," I said.

"Where did you last see them?"

"I had them when I drove home after dinner," I said. "But I can't for the life of me remember what I did with them after that."

"That's easily taken care of, Will. What time did you get home?"

"About 6:30."

"Well, then, I'll just fly back through the time barrier and see what you did with them."

"But Splendid Man, if you tamper with the past, couldn't that screw up the future somehow?"

"No, Will," he said. "I've tried before to change the course of history, but it just doesn't work. Like the time I zipped back through the time barrier and tried to stop the Gulf of Tonkin incident and thus prevent the escalation of the Vietnam War. We know how that turned out. And besides, I'll merely be observing the past, not tampering with it."

"Okay then," I said. "If you don't mind."

Splendid Man vanished in a blur and reappeared instants later. "Look in the garbage, Will," he said.

I did so, and sure enough, under the Burger King bag, there were my keys.

"I went back and saw that you'd let so much trash accumulate in your car," said Splendid Man, "that when you carried it all upstairs, your keys got mixed in with it."

"Thanks, pal," I said. "Listen, I hope you don't mind me using my SOS Comb for something this insignificant."

"Certainly not. Feel free to summon me with your SOS Comb for any reason, not only because you've fallen off a tall building, have undergone a bizarre physical transformation, or are menaced by a motorcycle gang. And the same goes for the toll-free number at my Citadel of Contemplation on the moon."

"Appreciate it, Splendid Man," I said. At the mention of his Citadel I felt a twinge of embarrassment about my own dumpy abode, but I figured if it didn't bother him I wouldn't let it bother me. "Hey, now that you're here, can you stay a while? Or do you have to run?"

"Fly, Will. I don't think I do, but let me take a quick check." He turned his body in a complete circle, holding his head at an odd angle. "Everything looks fine. There is a comet hurtling toward Earth, but I see that my Canadian pal, Northern Light, is already zipping off to dispatch it with his power medallion."

"That's great," I said, heading for the kitchen to mix a couple of drinks. "Why don't you take a load off and we'll talk."

"I'd love to, Will," he said, "but on one condition."

"What's that, Splendid Man?"

"That you knock off this 'Splendid Man' business. Aren't we good enough friends yet that you can stop addressing me by my title?"

"Sure thing…Cal," I said with a grin, using the short form of his native Strontiumese name.

When I returned to the living room Cal was sitting on my parents' old couch and scanning the bookshelves that dominated my modest living room. He took a sip of his Manhattan and asked, "So, Will, are there any more books you can recommend for me to read?"

"*More* books!" I said, my mouth agape. Just last week I'd recommended the entire Britannica Great Books series to him. "You don't mean you've already read every volume you were interested in!"

"I've already read every volume, Will. Period. Haven't I mentioned that, in addition to physical Splendid Speed, the argon-tinged atmosphere and lesser gravity of Earth grant astounding mental speed to all Strontiumese?"

He had, in fact, mentioned that, and in precisely those words. But I still couldn't get used to it. "And I guess Splendid Vision really helps navigate that tiny print," I grinned.

"That it does," he said, in complete earnest. "And I must say, I enjoyed every page of every book."

I was afraid he would say that. Teaching the big lug some discernment was not turning out to be easy. "Okay," I said carefully. "But surely you must have enjoyed some more than others?"

He took another sip of his Manhattan, a slow one this time, and I sensed him stalling. For the first time I saw nervousness in those glacier-blue eyes. "Well, of course, I'm no expert..."

"Just tell me what you think, Cal. No one expects you to be a connoisseur of literature yet."

He breathed an audible sigh of relief. "I appreciate that, Will. I'm a bit gun shy after all the razzing I've taken from Catman, that calico-cowled nemesis of crime, about my taste in books. That's why I value the way you've taken me under your wing. Metaphorically speaking."

I caught a twinkle in his eye. Before he met me, he would never have been talking about metaphors. "Don't mention it, Cal. I'm used to loaning books to friends and having them return them months later only half read. It's a pleasure to have a pal who actually reads what I recommend."

"Oh, and I'm starting to get a lot out of them!" he said eagerly. "I thought I knew all about truth and justice until I read those Plato volumes."

"I had a feeling you'd like the Greeks," I said. "They appreciated the heroic."

"And what playwrights! I had no idea great literature could be so entertaining. I laughed so hard reading Aristophanes's *Frogs* that I would have busted a gut, if my internal organs, like my bodily exterior, were not invulnerable. Do you have anything else by him?"

"I wish I did. But that volume includes all his surviving works."

"Surviving?" he asked. "You mean some of them have been lost to the winds of time?"

"You could put it that way. All the great Greek dramatists—the tragedians Aeschylus, Sophocles, and Euripides and the comedians Aristophanes and Menander—have been shown to have written far more works than still survive. Ditto for Plato, Aristotle, and the other classical philosophers. One of the great calamities of ancient history was the unexplained destruction by fire of the great library of Alexandria during Caesar's campaign in 48 B.C., which resulted in the eternal loss of innumerable classics of literature and philosophy."

"Great Amundsen, Will!" he exclaimed, rising from his seat. "I had no idea! What a tragedy! All those lost works must have been magnificent. One thing I've noticed is that those ancient authors never seemed to write a bad book."

"Of course not," I grumbled. "They were fortunate enough to live in an era when economics and art were in harmony, and an author was encouraged to be true to his vision. They didn't have to contend with a short-sighted commercial publishing 'industry' devoted to snuffing the literary soul."

"Why, Will," he gasped, "I've never heard you sound so bitter! Have you suffered another setback in your own literary career?"

"You could put it that way." I explained to him how I'd hit a creative wall in the middle of Chapter 38 of my new novel and how what I'd thought would be the consummation of my years of writing looked doomed to end up as just another item in my trunk.

"Now, Will, you shouldn't give up so quickly," he said. "You're only twenty-six years old, which I understand is quite young for a writer. And don't you think your whole perspective on your work will change once you've succeeded in getting published?"

"Published!" I snorted. "What good is getting published if it means betraying my own vision to cater to the blind editors of New

York? Even the writers who start out great are seduced into prostituting themselves in this modern world. Look at Norman Mailer! Tennessee Williams! Harold Robbins!"

"But Will. I thought you told me that Harold Robbins has always been bad."

"That's beside the point," I muttered.

He sat back down, took a swig of his drink, and looked at me with grave concern. "It sounds to me, pal," he said, "as though what you need is some inspiration. Nothing lifts me out of the doldrums of self-doubt like remembering the sacrifices of the great heroes of the past. That's why I keep life-size statues of Hercules, Samson, and Eleanor Roosevelt in my Citadel of Contemplation."

"It's different with you. You can defeat Cerebriac as he plunders an alien planet in exactly the way a hero of the past did and people will say, 'What a hero! Splendid Man is the new Robin Hood!' If I use someone else's plot they'll say, 'What a plagiarist! Will Jones is the new Jerzy Kosinski!'"

"But Will, didn't you tell me yourself that every writer draws from the classics? That, for example, Robert Penn Warren's *All the King's Men* is a Sophoclean tragedy in the costume of the Jim Crow South?"

"Words to that effect, anyway," I grumbled. "But the last thing the world needs is another reworking of *Oedipus*."

"Fair enough," he said, with a shrewd glint in his eye. "But what if you were to draw your inspiration from a classic that no one else living has read? Say, one of the lost works of the Athenian dramatists?"

"Swell. Except where the hell am I going to read plays that have been lost for centuries?"

"Centuries *ago*, that's where!" He grinned and slapped my knee. "Didn't you say they had them all in stock in the library of ancient Alexandria?"

It took me a few seconds, but then I got it. "Of course! Your Splendid Speed can break the time barrier! You can actually go to ancient Alexandria!"

"Oh, I've already gone, several times. But I have to confess I haven't once stopped by the library. I guess I assumed that since I didn't reside there, I could never be issued a library card."

"Then, for heaven's sake, you've got to go read those ancient dramas!" I yelled. "And as soon as you come back to the present you'll have to stop by and tell me what they're all about."

"I have a better idea, Will. We can just zip off to 48 B.C. together and you can have a look around for yourself!"

"Me? Go with you?" I gulped. "But wouldn't I be...I don't know..."

"Buffeted to death by the temporal winds that rage along the time stream?" he asked.

"Exactly!" I said.

"Oh no, Will. I wouldn't let that happen to you. I'll just wrap you in my indestructible cape, as I do with my pal Bobby Anderssen, that albino cub reporter, take you under my arm, and fly you there safe and sound."

I jumped to my feet. "Then let's go!"

One moment I was looking through my window at the gloomy skies and cookie-cutter apartment houses of San Francisco's Richmond District, and the next I was looking at utter darkness. Bundled securely in Splendid Man's cape I was unable to hear, see, or smell the passage of eons as we hurtled back through time. It was a lot like a sensory deprivation tank, I thought, only different.

Suddenly Splendid Man unwrapped the cape from around my head. The sun glinted on the blue Mediterranean below us. On a small island towered a massive stone structure, undoubtedly the Lighthouse of Alexandria, one of the seven wonders of the ancient world. And on the coast a great city came into view: Alexandria herself, intellectual center of Hellenistic civilization!

Despite the awe-inspiring sights, an irrelevant thought crossed my mind as Splendid Man landed in the great agora in the city center, a thought that I nevertheless felt compelled to voice.

"Tell me, Cal, is your hair invulnerable too? I've noticed that despite the velocities we attain on our flights, it never looks mussed."

"Why yes, Will, of course it's invulnerable," he replied. "But you must understand that not even invulnerable hair will stay in place against the buffeting it withstands at interstellar speeds. That's why I use a little dab of Brylcreem every morning. It even keeps my forelock in place."

We wafted down behind a temple, just out of sight of the city's crowds. Since everyone I saw was clad in a white robe or toga, I felt a bit conspicuous in my mock turtleneck and jeans. But taking my cue from Cal, who didn't seem remotely self-conscious even in his gleaming gold tights and crimson cape, I plunged into the teeming streets of Alexandria.

Even as I tried to soak up every sight and sound around me, I couldn't help looking ahead for evidence of the great library. My heart was pounding in anticipation of the lost literary masterworks that I, Will Jones, would soon find laid before me. And from those masterworks, who knew what flood of novelistic brilliance would pour from my newly inflamed soul and what success would follow? I could already picture myself giving notice to my manager at 7-Eleven!

"I hope we've landed at the right time," I said. "I'd hate to have come here after the library had already burned."

"Well, we'll just have to ask one of the friendly locals."

"Don't tell me you speak Ancient Greek."

"With my power of Splendid Recall, I'm able to be fluent in quite a number of languages, Will. Over six thousand on Earth alone, in fact. And, by carefully manipulating the powers of my Splendid Voice, I'll make sure to provide translations of everything as we go. I know how uncomfortable it feels to stand by while people converse in a language you can't understand. That happened to me once with the sponge beings of Procyon 3. Boy, is that a tough language to crack!"

"I'll take your word for it," I said.

Splendid Man stepped up to a merchant dressed in a toga with a laurel wreath set in his curly blond locks. And sure enough, I heard a simultaneous translation of the conversation as if it were being whispered in my ear. "Excuse me, Citizen," said Cal, "can you tell two travelers what year this is?"

"What kind of question is that?" responded the merchant. "It's 48 B.C., of course!"

With a yelp of glee I hurried on, pulling Cal after me.

But as we rounded a corner, the sight of billowing black smoke stopped us in our tracks. Splendid Man sniffed the air with his Splendid Smell and said, "That's peculiar, Will. That smells like a gasoline fire to me—and yet gasoline hadn't yet been refined in this period of history."

Without another word he caught me under his arm and took to the air. We saw wine-colored flames licking at the marble walls, the broad stairway, and the classical columns of a great building, above the door of which was inscribed, "Alexandria Public Library." It was too late for even Splendid Man's powers to make a difference.

Simultaneously, Splendid Man and I spotted a figure wearing a white lab smock and lacking eyebrows, hurrying away with a two-gallon Chevron can clutched in his hand.

"Why, that's my archfoe, the evil scientist Pox Pascal!" exclaimed Splendid Man. "So he's responsible for the unexplained destruction of the Library of Alexandria!"

Splendid Man changed direction, but before he could swoop down on the smooth-browed villain, Pascal climbed into a time bubble that he had hidden behind some olive trees and vanished into the time stream. Defeated, we watched the building crumble before our eyes.

"Is there nothing we can do?" I asked.

Splendid Man's brow was furrowed in thought. "Yes, Will, there is one thing we can do. We can travel a little further back in time and be here waiting for Pascal when he arrives."

"Great," I sighed. "And we can go back a little further, can't we? To give us time to read a few plays?"

"Tragedies, comedies, philosophical dialogues, you name it, pal! And since we're going back only a short time, we won't need to take to the air to get there. Borrowing a tip from my friend Quickie, the Swiftest Man Alive, I can vibrate at Splendid Speed and break the time barrier while apparently standing still."

He took hold of me and vibrated, and I watched the flames die down and the building rise up again before my eyes, as if by a trick of cinematography. Suddenly we were standing before the library in all its splendor. We ascended the stairs expectantly and passed through the mighty doors.

The library was actually only one part of a larger complex called a museum—though "museum" was meant in the ancient sense, denoting an institute of study. There were wings for mathematics, astronomy, and medicine. We passed a botanical garden and a menagerie. The latter reminded me somewhat of Splendid Man's menagerie in his Citadel of Contemplation, only I didn't spot any species from other star systems.

Suddenly a sculpture caught my eye. It was of Aphrodite. And brother, anybody who says the ancient Greeks were all gay needs to brush up on his scholarship! I promise you, whoever set his chisel to this honey's curves wasn't thinking about Spartan warriors wrestling in olive oil! For a minute I even thought of asking Cal if he knew any Hellenistic girls he could fix me up with. But then I remembered that long distance relationships hardly ever work out.

I'd started to walk away before I realized that Splendid Man wasn't beside me. Looking back, I saw that he had stopped at another statue, although not of a goddess. He was gazing at a marble nude of a male Olympic athlete. After a long moment he said thoughtfully, "Those Greeks had a very healthy attitude about…things. Didn't they, Will?"

"Well, if you mean they were free of Victorian hypocrisies about the nude in art," I said, "then you're absolutely right."

For an instant he looked as though he were about to correct me, but then he caught himself. He gave me a long look, then he nodded and said quietly, "Yes, of course, Will. That's exactly what I meant."

"That's a great observation, Cal!" I said, and I'll confess I felt a swell of pride. When the big guy had first asked me to help him become more cultured, I'd had my doubts. But under my guidance he was starting to show sides of himself that I'd never imagined were there.

At last we entered the library itself. We discovered, however, that it wasn't easy finding the books we were looking for, since the Dewey Decimal System hadn't been invented yet. Failing even to find an author and title catalogue, we sought out the librarian. An elderly woman in a frumpy toga, her hair drawn back into a bun, sat at the Returned Scrolls counter.

"Excuse me, ma'am," whispered Splendid Man, once again translating for me as he went. "We're looking for the later works of the great Athenian dramatists and philosophers of the Age of Pericles."

"Right this way, please," she said. She led us down shelves of scrolls arranged into the popular Greek genres: Epics, Odes, Gnomic Elegies, Dithyrambs. She patted a shelf and said, "The Drama section is here. You'll find Philosophy around the corner, next to Sports Stories."

We plunged into the scrolls. Going alphabetically, we came first upon Aeschylus. Splendid Man translated the titles from the Greek as he read. "*Agamemnon...The Eumenides....* Oh, here's one that wasn't in the Great Books, Will. It's called, *I, the Tribunal.*"

"Wha—?" I exclaimed. "Can you scan it and see what it's about?"

"I'll do better than that, Will. I'll read the whole thing at Splendid Speed and condense it for you." He flipped through the scroll at a blur and said, "It's about a vengeance-crazed Spartan mercenary and his many encounters with corrupt, beautiful women and vicious hoods."

"My God," I said. "That's...that's terrible!"

"Why is that, Will?"

"It sounds like a Mickey Spillane book!"

"Well, I enjoyed it," Splendid Man said. "It's true that that his grammar isn't as good as it was in his earlier works, but it certainly was fast-paced."

"Forget it," I muttered. "Read something else."

"Here's Aristophanes. Goodness, that fellow wrote a lot, didn't he?"

"Do you see any lost works?"

"I sure do, pal," he said, already speed-reading a scroll. "Wow! I can see you doing something really great with this plot!"

"What is it?"

"It's called *Barefoot in the Agora.* It's a light domestic comedy about newlyweds in the big city of Athens."

"Oh, Lord," I said.

"What's wrong, Will? I thought you'd be more excited."

"Let's try again," I said. "I know Euripides won't let us down."

Splendid Man looked and said, "Here's one. It's called *Platonic Story.*"

"No!" I gasped.

He zipped through the scroll and reported, "It's a nice love story about two students who meet at the Platonic Academy."

"Let me guess. One of them dies at the end from an incurable disease."

"How'd you know?" asked Splendid Man.

"Move along," I said. "Move along."

The rest were no different: Menander's *Blazing Chariots* and Sophocles's *Island of the Dolls*. I crumpled against the shelves in despair. "I can't believe it," I moaned. "How could they do it? How could they throw it all away for a quick buck?"

"Will, didn't you tell me once that all the basic plots of Western literature are contained within the works of the Greek dramatists?" asked Cal. "Couldn't they just have run out of good stories?"

I glared at him.

"Well, I'm sorry you didn't find anything to inspire you," he said. "Maybe we should move to the Philosophy section. Didn't you tell me there's always consolation in classical philosophy?"

That I had, and as we rounded Sports Stories and came upon shelves filled to bursting with copious scrolls, I felt my spirits rise a little. For I, Will Jones, was about to become the first modern man—or at least the first modern, non-Splendid-Powered man—to discover the lost works of the men who had forged the consciousness of the West.

"Here's something by Aristotle I don't recognize," he said, unrolling a long scroll.

"Aristotle," I said in hushed tones. "The greatest mind of the ancient world."

"Yes. It's called *How to Prosper During the Coming Plague.*"

An anguished groan escaped my lips. "Put it down! I don't want to know any more!"

"But here's the Plato section!"

"No, Cal! Don't look at it!"

"But you love Plato, Will. And here's one I've never heard of before. Don't you want to know what it's called?"

I couldn't help myself. After all, it was Plato, the fountainhead of Western thought. "Okay," I said. "Shoot."

"Attaboy, Will," he said. "It's called *The Sensuous Catamite.* Would you like to know what it's about?"

"No!" I screamed. "Let's just get out of here!"

As I dragged him toward the exit, Splendid Man said, "Aren't you being a little harsh on your fellow writers, Will? Some of those philosophy tips were awfully useful. And those plays were sure entertaining."

"Catman was right," I said. "You've still got a lot to learn about literature, Splendid Man."

"But I don't understand, Will. What exactly is it that distinguishes high art from hack work?"

"It's not something I can put into words, Cal. Ernest Hemingway expressed it best. He said that you just have to have a built-in, shockproof shit detector."

"Will!" exclaimed Cal, aghast. "There are children here!"

He hurried me outside. As we stood on the steps, he sniffed the air. "I smell gasoline again," he said.

"Pascal must have arrived via his time bubble," I said.

Before the words were out of my mouth, tongues of flame were darting around us. Splendid Man reacted instantly, using his Splendid Suction to rob the flames of oxygen and snuff them. I saw black dots swirling before my eyes, but then he exhaled and I could breathe again.

Pascal appeared from around the corner of the museum. "Splendid Man!" he gasped. "How ironic that we should meet thousands of years in our past for our final showdown!"

"Fiend!" snarled Splendid Man. "How could you try to deprive the world of one of its great treasure troves of literature?"

"The world will be better off!" hissed Pascal. "If not for me, every classical scholar on earth would be crushed by disillusionment at the spectacle of the world's greatest writers disgracing themselves! Without me, what would become of the world's intelligentsia?" With that, he drew a glowing silver rock from under his shirt, tossed it at Splendid Man's feet, and ran for his time bubble.

As Splendid Man crumpled groaning to his knees beside me, I realized that the rock must be strontiumite, one of those space-borne fragments of his lost planet that are deadly to him but harmless to earthlings. Which meant it was all up to me. I hurled the glowing rock at Pascal. My years as a Little League pitcher paid off, because it struck him smack on the back of his head.

"Good toss, Will!" said Splendid Man as he apprehended Pascal and pushed him into his time bubble. "This will teach you, Pascal, that no matter how well educated we may be, none of us has the right to decide which books will or will not be read by succeeding generations! That's the democratic way!"

With one hand, Splendid Man hurled the time bubble into space, explaining, "I'm sending Pascal on a little trip through time and space. Thanks to my Splendid Aim, he'll materialize back in our own time, orbiting the moon. Later I'll retrieve him and return him to the maximum-security penitentiary where he belongs."

As he vanished into the sky, we heard Pascal calling, "We'll meet again, Splendid Man, for our final showdown!"

Splendid Man turned to me and said, "Although he is a twisted, diabolical genius, Pascal does have a love for the finer things in life. That love has made him a hero on the argon-free planet Poxor where, ironically, I am looked upon as a villain."

Suddenly the elderly librarian rushed down the stairs, waving a slip of parchment in her hand.

"I saw what you did for us, young man!" she said to Cal. "And as a token of appreciation, I'd like to present you with this honorary library card to our wonderful library, the center of learning in the Hellenistic world!"

Splendid Man's face lit up when he said, "I'm truly honored, ma'am. I'll give this card a place of honor beside my many trophies of past adventures in my 20th Century Citadel of Contemplation."

We waved goodbye, and Splendid Man flew us to a nearby hilltop for one last look at this glorious city. As we gazed in awe at this monument of civilization, he put his arm around me. Suddenly, by an ironic twist of fate, a lightning bolt cleaved the clear blue sky and struck the museum. The great building burst into flames.

Splendid Man twitched beside me, but he made no effort to fly down and combat the blaze.

"Splendid Man!" I cried. "Why don't you do something?"

"Because it was meant to be, Will," he said. "As I explained before, not even a Splendid Man can alter the course of history."

"How tragic," I said. But I have to confess that I was secretly thinking it was probably just as well. I never would have guessed it could happen, and I certainly wasn't going to mention it to my heroic pal, but on this one I actually found myself agreeing with Pox Pascal.

Splendid Man looked awfully glum as he wrapped me in his cape for our return to the present. "I hope you're not too disappointed that this trip to the past amounted to nothing, pal," he said.

"Well," I said, "I'll admit that I was at first. But I hope you know that I'm not in this friendship in the hopes of benefiting from your Splendid Powers. It was worth it just to have this time together, even if I am still as stuck as ever on Chapter 38 of my novel."

"I'm glad to hear you say that, Will. And I want you to know that, even though my Splendid Powers turned out to be of no use to you, your own Splendid Knowledge of history and culture was a huge boon to me."

I didn't get the chance to thank him for that, because just then his cape closed over my face and we hurtled into the time stream.

Episode Two
The Girl in the Canned City

The doorbell startled me. I'd been sitting in my room catching up on my self-pity, and the last thing I'd expected was a visitor. I threw open my door and blinked.

"Well," I said. "I sure didn't figure to find you in my hall. Especially in that get-up." I was referring to the conservative blue business suit that Cal is so often shown wearing in the comic books but which I'd never seen on him in person. "Come in, come in."

"Long time no see, Will," he said, brushing past me into my apartment. Even in the dull clothes I had to admit he was a perfect specimen of manhood. Of course, next to my five-feet seven and a hundred-and-twenty pounds most men look like perfect specimens of manhood.

"Would you like a drink?" I asked.

"What have you got?"

"Only bourbon and soda, I'm afraid. I hope you like highballs."

"I love highballs," he said.

"Good. Have a seat and I'll be right with you."

With his usual selflessness, he lowered himself onto my sagging couch, leaving the one good chair for me. I mixed the drinks and handed one to him. "So, what brings you by, Cal?"

He took a sip and said, "You'd better call me Ken as long as I'm dressed like this, Will. You never know, one of my enemies, like Giganto the Splendid Mandrill or the Hideous Thing from 1,000,000 A.D., may have seen us together and bugged your apartment. Certainly 'Cal' is safer than my full Strontiumese name Calv'In, but even so, if they overheard you they might tumble to my secret identity."

"Ken. I just can't get used to calling you that." I'd been stumbling over the name since the night we'd gone out for pizza and he'd divulged his secret identity. I was about to inquire again as to the nature of his visit but I stopped myself. I realized that with his power of Splendid Recall my question would come back to him soon, and he'd answer me when he was good and ready.

Sure enough, a moment later he said, "I just thought I'd drop in, Will. You haven't summoned me with your SOS Comb for such a long time that I was getting worried about you."

"It's nothing," I said, and before I knew what I was doing I was pulling a pack of cigarettes out of my pocket. I was embarrassed that I'd started smoking again, but you know how it is when you're in a funk. "I've just been working through some personal issues and I didn't want to burden you with them."

"Let me have one of those," Splendid Man said.

It took me a second, but then I realized he meant the cigarettes. "Don't tell me you smoke," I said.

"Although I can live interminably without food and drink," he explained, "I find I need a little tobacco now and then. It helps me think." He took a cigarette and set it between his lips. I offered him my lighter, but he waved it away and lit the cigarette with the heat setting of his Splendid Vision.

"I hope I'm not giving you my bad habits," I said.

"Don't be silly, Will. Friends always pick up one another's habits and attributes."

"Depends on how you look at it, Ken. Have I started flying at interstellar speed, stopping bullets with my indestructible chest, or battling such menaces as the cybernetic space villain Cerebriac?"

"No," Splendid Man said. "But you certainly are picking up my speech patterns."

"Heaven forbid," I said.

"Now what's this tomfoolery about not burdening me with your problems?" he said, blowing a perfect smoke ring that spiraled toward the ceiling like a celestial body. "You and Bobby Anderssen, that albino cub reporter, are my best pals. I'm only delighted to help you with your problems, like the time Bobby turned into a giant abalone-man and I helped him by telepathically summoning my old mermaid sweetheart Pura Poseidonis and her friends in Lemuria to find the cause of his bizarre transformation."

"Yeah, I know, Ken. But you've got more important things to do than play psychologist to me."

"What's the problem, Will? I insist."

I shrugged and looked at my feet. "I've just been feeling lonely of late."

"Great Amundsen, Will! What do you expect? You never get out of the house, except to go to work. And you're never going to meet people in your job as a security guard at a self-storage facility. All you do in your time off is read and write. Don't get me wrong. I think the literary life is very honorable. You know that. You know how much I enjoy our literary talks. But there's more to life than books and comics. You've got to get out more. Meet more people. Try different activities."

"I know that, Ken. Don't you think I know that? But Christ, sometimes you get into such a deep rut that it feels like you'll never climb out again."

Without another word, Cal stood up and in the twinkling of an eye stripped off his outer garments to reveal himself in his gold tights, red cape, and red boots. He compressed his blue suit into the pouch in his cape with his Splendid Strength and said, "What you need is a change of scene, Will. So put out your cigarette and we'll go on a little trip."

"Where to?" I asked.

"First to my Citadel of Contemplation on the moon," he said. "Then you'll see. Now open a window and let's get going."

"Why don't we just stay here? *Picnic*'s on TV tonight. It's one of my favorite movies."

"Great Amundsen! You really are in bad shape."

That got to me. It's one thing to know yourself that your life is a mess, but when somebody you respect agrees with you, then you really feel lousy. I crushed my butt, drew back the curtains, and opened the window wide.

Cal had removed his cape. He wrapped me in it from head to

toe and put an arm around me to lift me into the air.

"Wait!" I said. "Won't I need a space suit, lest the vacuum of outer space cause my non-invulnerable body to hyperinflate?"

"You see?" he said. "You are beginning to talk like me."

"Okay," I said. "Won't I blow the fuck up in space?"

"Only if we dawdle, Will," he said.

Well, let me tell you, *he* didn't dawdle. One moment I felt us taking to the skies and the next we were landing on the moon. There was a dicey moment while I waited for him to unlock the door to his Citadel of Contemplation with the giant key he'd disguised as an American flag, but it didn't take him more than half a second, not nearly long enough for me to blow the fuck up. Then we were wafting down into the bowels of the unearthly structure.

Splendid Man's citadel is actually a generation starship that Strontium had launched decades before its destruction by a cataclysmic flood. Something had gone horribly wrong (which, if science fiction stories are any guide, seems to be pretty standard for generation starships), and all hands had perished except for Cal's cousin Kar'En. Cal had discovered the ship just in time to rescue her before her air gave out. She, of course, went on to become Splendid Girl, and he buried the gargantuan ship on the moon, gradually refitting it into his home away from home.

Even though he'd brought me here a few times before, I was still flabbergasted by all his trophies from different worlds, his intergalactic menagerie, and his scientific gadgetry. This time, though, maybe because I was getting a little bit used to the place, I was also struck by other details I'd never noticed before. Walls of mauve and saffron. Tasteful area lighting that accented a pair of Erté statuettes of women in flamboyant gowns. Handsomely framed posters of *Cabaret* and *A Chorus Line.*

I made a mental note to ask him sometime if a skill for interior decorating was a legacy of Strontiumese culture or another of the Splendid Powers he had developed on Earth. Although how argon or lesser gravity could affect a guy's aesthetic sense I couldn't imagine.

I followed him through several rooms, admiring the life-size statues of Catman and Sparrow, both in costume and in their identities as Wyatt Brewster and his ward, Greg Dickson, his library, which includes for the most part titles I've recommended, and finally the room containing Strontor, the City in a Can. It became clear what Cal had meant by a change of scene when he brought out a couple of parachutes. I, Will Jones, was about to visit the sole surviving city of Splendid Man's native world, which the cybernetic space criminal Cerebriac had shrunk (also before the aforementioned flood) and imprisoned in a can.

"Wow," I said. "I sure feel honored."

He smiled and instructed me to place on my head a metal cap connected by wires to a bizarre apparatus on the wall.

"This machine," he explained, throwing a switch, "will enable you to speak fluent Strontiumese in moments."

"You're putting me on," I said, and realized as soon as the words had left my mouth that I'd spoken in a strange, alien tongue.

"Its effect is only temporary," he said, also speaking in Strontiumese, which I understood perfectly, "but it will certainly last you through your visit. Okay, you can take it off now."

"Amazing," I said. "I can't believe it."

"It's one thing to understand Strontiumese," he said, "but quite another to speak it. You won't have any problems though, because, being fluent in Spanish, it's a cinch for you to roll your R's. Bobby has a heck of a time."

The next part of the operation startled me. Splendid Man turned on the shrinking ray and in instants we dwindled to the size of gnats—clothes, parachutes, and all. Then he put his arm around my shoulders and up and away we went toward the now-distant top of the can. "As you well know," he explained on the way, "I lose all my Splendid Powers in Strontor, the City in a Can, and so I, too, have to parachute down."

"Of course," I said. "And I'll have to be fitted with special shoes when we get there in order to withstand the terrible gravitational pull of Strontor."

He raised his eyebrows. "Why Will, where did you learn that? I don't remember telling you about it."

"I read about in the comics, Cal. Bobby always needs special shoes when you bring him to Strontor."

"Of course, Will. I'd forgotten you were such a scrupulous reader of AC/DC Comics."

We'd finally gotten to the top of the can and we approached one of the many air holes. I saw that the hole was covered with what looked like a grating to my tiny eyes, but which I realized must be the filter that removes the trace argon from Earth's atmosphere. "Say, Cal," I asked, "what effects can I expect from breathing argon-free air? Oddly, that never seems to be addressed in the comics."

"Just a slight tightening of the scrotum, Will. Nothing to worry about."

"Okay," I said, "not so odd."

Splendid Man waved me back and, kneeling down, peered over the edge of the air hole. "We're in luck," he said. "Strontor's artificial sun isn't in our path of descent."

"That's nice," I said.

He motioned me forward. "Don't look down," he cautioned. "In our present size the drop is awesome. Just jump in, count to ten, and open your chute."

I followed directions, not daring to look down until my chute had ballooned about me and I was gently wafting down. But even then it was quite a shock. We were much higher over the city below than any jet plane ever gets above the surface of the earth. Relatively speaking, that is.

Cal, being more experienced at this sort of thing than I, had timed the opening of his chute so that we descended side by side.

"Do you like it?" he asked.

"It's fantastic!" I exclaimed. We were close enough to the city now that it began to take on distinctive contours. It was mind-boggling to find myself in such an exotic setting when from the outside it looked like a restaurant-size can of pork and beans. "Strontor looks a lot like San Francisco," I said. "Only different."

"I'm glad you appreciate things like that, Will," he said.

"That's one of the reasons I value your friendship."

That reminded me. "Hey, Cal," I said, "let me ask you a question."

"Sure, Will."

"You remember when I told you my middle name?"

"Why, of course I do, Will. It was the same night I divulged my secret identity to you."

"Exactly. It was no coincidence that that's when you really decided you could trust me as a friend, was it?"

"Well, no, I have to confess that it wasn't. As you must know from the comics, an odd quirk of fate has thrown me over and over again into intimate contact with people bearing double P's in their names. Pepper Pine, Patti Pert, Pura Poseidonis, and Pox Pascal, to name but a few. Of course, I already valued our literary discussions, but that alone isn't enough to form a basis for a genuine friendship. I'll admit that the discovery that you had two P's in your middle name made me feel instantly closer to you than I would have to, say, Saul Bellow or even Walker Percy."

Through the rest of our descent, I reflected on how glad I was that, despite my father's desire to call me William James Jones, thus naming me after a great philosopher and a fine novelist at once, my mother had stuck to her guns and insisted on Chipper.

As soon as we touched ground, a delegation of Strontorians gathered around us. A maiden fell to her knees and replaced my boots with special gravity shoes. She had stooped so quickly that I hadn't gotten a look at her face, but something about her seemed strangely familiar.

"People of Strontor," said Splendid Man to the crowd, "this is my friend Will Jones, from San Francisco."

An elderly man in a green headband stepped forward and said, "Yes, we have monitored San Francisco on our screens. It looks a lot like Strontor, only different. And a lot bigger."

After him, a young man in a red headband who looked remarkably like Splendid Man addressed me, "Our screens reveal that you're a writer, Will."

"Well," I said uncomfortably, "I do like to write."

Just then the maiden finished buckling the shoes to my feet and stood before me. I nearly choked when I saw her. "Ellen!" I gasped. "What are you doing in Strontor?"

She looked mystified. Cal chuckled. Then I remembered. Through another of fate's odd quirks, many Strontorians are the exact physical doubles of people on Earth. The comic books mentioned doubles of Pepper Pine, Bobby Anderssen, Patti Pert, and blustering newspaper editor Oliver Hazard Black, so it should have been no surprise to find myself face to face with a double of Ellen, my ex-fiancée. Except that I'd had no idea there were Jews on Strontium.

Cal was looking at me with a peculiar glint in his eyes. He said hastily, "Will, I have to pay a visit to some scientist friends of mine who are working on a ray to restore Strontor to its original size. I'll leave you in the capable hands of Jen'Ee here."

"Well...er...I..." I began, but before I could complete my protest he had waved and turned his back and left me alone with Jen'Ee.

I had thought that in the two years since my fiancée had left me I had gotten over her. But now, in the presence of her Strontorian double, I began to have my doubts. I suddenly understood how Monroe Stahr must have felt in *The Last Tycoon*. It made me wonder if Splendid Man had ever brought Scott Fitzgerald to Strontor. But it seemed unlikely, since Fitzgerald didn't have any P's in his name. Not to mention that he'd been dead long before Splendid Man was even born.

"Would you like me to take you on a tour of our canned city?" Jen'Ee asked.

"That would be nice, El...er...Jen'Ee," I said.

She showed me the great statue of Splendid Man in Strontor Square, the monitor rooms, and the laboratories filled with ultrascientific Strontorian inventions. We walked the streets and I gaped at the flying cars, the glass-walled domiciles raised on columns, the amazingly humanoid robots. It reminded me of the world of the Jetsons.

Despite the special gravity shoes, I found my feet hurting by the time we had walked through the whole downtown. Not to mention the rather uncomfortable tightening of the scrotum that I was experiencing. I spotted a bar and suggested we go in for a drink.

"I'd love to," she said.

We sat by the window and watched Strontor's artificial sun sink behind the futuristic domes and spires of the city. I wondered where it went. I beckoned to the waitress, who looked amazingly like my landlady, and Jen'Ee ordered the drinks, since I was unfamiliar with Strontiumese mixology.

What with all the things to gape at, I'd hardly spoken three words to Jen'Ee, and she'd been too busy playing the tour guide to say much of a personal nature to me. But for all the marvels of the canned city that she'd laid at my feet, it was she who had captivated me. They say looks aren't everything, but try putting that to the test if you ever find yourself in the presence of a woman who's an exact double of the one true love of your life!

Our drinks arrived. They were two tall glasses of frothing green liquid with golden globules floating inside.

"What do you think?" she asked, as I sipped mine tentatively.

"Interesting," I said. "It tastes a lot like Tang."

"What is that?"

"An advanced beverage developed by Earth's scientists for the use of astronauts. Maybe someday, once Calv'In and his scientific friends perfect their enlarging ray, you can come visit me on Earth and try some."

She averted her eyes and stammered, "I…I'd love to. But I'm afraid I can never leave Strontor, the City in a Can. It's my home."

What a contrast, I thought, to my ex-fiancée Ellen, whose restlessness had driven her from the canned city of our life into the bigger world beyond, in search of herself.

"But maybe you could live in Strontor for a while," she said. "Being bilingual, I'm sure you could find a job."

"It's tempting," I said. "As stimulating as I find San Francisco, I've often thought I'd be happier living someplace smaller." I paused and added, "I trust that if I do decide to live here, I'll be able to keep seeing you."

"Of course," she said softly.

We left the bar and strolled through the twilit streets of Strontor. I saw dead ringers for Mickey Mantle, Ayatollah Khomeini, and Floyd the barber. I took Jen'Ee's hand and she didn't snatch it away. She offered to show me more of Strontor's technological miracles. I suggested we take in an art gallery instead.

"Art?" she said, and looked confused for a minute. "Oh, wait. I know what you mean now. Paintings and things, right? I'm afraid we haven't had those on Strontor since the advancement of science rendered culture obsolete."

I felt a cold hand grip my throat. "Then how about we go someplace where we can listen to some music?"

Her head titled to the side and she looked at me searchingly, much the way a dog does when it's trying to understand what you've said to it. At last she said, "Music?"

The cold hand tightened. For lack of a better idea, I suggested we return to the monitor rooms. I'd glanced at my watch and seen that is was almost 8:30.

Three hoary-bearded scientists in gray headbands were tending the monitor screens.

"What would you like to monitor, Mr. Jones?" asked one. "The Great Pyramids of Egypt?"

"Or would you rather see the Marianas Trench, the deepest point in all the world's oceans?" chimed another.

The third smiled kindly and said, "Or better yet, perhaps you'd like to see the famous frozen leopard carcass high on the snowy peak of Mount Kilimanjaro."

"Actually," I said, "I was wondering if you could tap into the satellite transmissions of KICU-TV in San Francisco."

Their hands flew to the dials, the screen flickered with wavy lines, and then *Picnic* came on the air.

We'd arrived just in time for my favorite scene. Everyone was at the Neewollah Ball, and Kim Novak and William Holden were about to begin their dance on the pier. As usual, I was completely enraptured by what I consider to be the most sensual scene in the history of cinema. But as soon as it was over I caught myself. What would Splendid Man think of me, spending my first evening in Strontor, the City in a Can, glued to the TV? Or monitor screen, as the case may be. How could I ignore the flesh-and-blood woman beside me in favor of a televised image, even if it was Kim Novak?

But when I turned to her and found her gazing at me with those puzzled eyes the knot formed in my throat again.

"Oh, Christ," I said. "Not movies, too?"

Although I was feeling dejected when we left the monitor rooms, I still held out one last hope. Art and music and movies were all well and good, I reflected, but I could live without them if I had to. There was one art form, however, that was nearer and dearer to me than life itself.

"Tell me, Jen'Ee," I said, and I heard the quaver in my voice. "Do you like to read?"

Oh, yes!" she exclaimed, and for a moment my heart soared. "I just finished reading a manual on the physics of anti-gravity."

"Yes, yes," I almost yelled. "But what about fiction?"

"Fiction?" she said, and when that look of incomprehension filled her face again I knew all was lost. Jen'Ee might have won my heart, but the city in the can was another story. For the first time I truly understood why Splendid Man, coming from where he had and bearing the DNA he bore, needed someone to tutor him in the arts.

As we turned onto a main street we saw Splendid Man emerge from a building, looking dejected.

"Cal! We're over here," I called.

He joined us on a street corner and said, "We failed again. We succeeded in enlarging a test group of Strontiumese rainbow mice, but after twenty minutes they reverted to savagery. I hate to think what would happen if we trained it on Strontorian humans."

"I'm sorry, Cal," I said, "That must be awfully disappointing."

"But that's not the worst of it, Will. I hate to tell you this, but there's a danger in remaining in Strontor. If you stay too long, the effects of the shrinking ray will become permanent and you'll be unable to return to your original size."

"How long do I have?" I asked.

"Ten minutes at the outside," he said. "Make it five. It'll take us that long to get to the airbase where our exit craft is waiting."

"Hey, wait a minute," I said. "You and Bobby have stayed here for weeks on end and he was always able to go back to his original size."

"That's true, Will. But during our experiments on the rainbow mice a ray escaped from the laboratory which mysteriously altered the atmosphere of Strontor, reducing the amount of time you can safely spend here. You have scarcely five minutes to decide whether you want to return to the outside world or stay here forever."

I turned around to face Jen'Ee. She looked at me with my fiancée's eyes, gave a little pout with lips that looked identical to those that had once said, "Yes." For a moment I thought of chucking it all and staying with her forever indeed. But suddenly the tightening in my scrotum became acute. Could I, Will Jones, live in a place where fiction didn't exist?

Jen'Ee seemed to sense my dilemma. She gave a sad little shrug and said, "Your place is out there, Will, in the world of fiction and culture and human passions. I had hoped we could get to know each other better, but I know you'd never be happy in the ultrascientific world of Strontor."

I nodded in resignation. Maybe it was true that I'd been in a terrible rut, but it was also true that the world of books and writing and, yes, comics, was the only world for me. We hugged in farewell. Then Cal put his hand on my shoulder to signal that we must go.

As the anti-gravity craft raised us toward the top of the can, I brooded on the unwelcome lesson I had learned tonight. Nothing, not the promise of a great love, not even the futuristic civilization of Strontor, the City in a Can, could tempt a writer to turn his back on his art.

Splendid Man interrupted my reverie. "You know, Will, it's really remarkable. This young lady Jen'Ee has an 'en' in her name, just as did not only your ex-fiancée Ellen, but your high-school sweetheart Maureen and that coworker you had a crush on, Henrietta. What an odd quirk of fate!"

"Yes," I sighed. "Isn't fate quirky?"

Episode Three
Will and Splendid Man's Double Date

"Tell me, Will. Often, when I read the liner notes in novels, I encounter the word 'Rabelaisian.' What exactly is meant by that?"

"Well, Cal, François Rabelais was a 16th Century French surgeon who wrote novels in his spare time. His work was characterized by ribald humor and gargantuan absurdity. So today, when a novelist displays those traits, he's often said to be Rabelaisian."

"But Will, that sounds like what you told me about Lawrence Sterne. Why don't we hear the word 'Sternian'?"

"Literary critics are a superstitious, cowardly lot," I said. "If one phrase catches on, the others are afraid to deviate from it."

"You know, that reminds me of the Ghost World, where Strontiumese criminals were exiled before the extinction of my people and now herd together like hyenas."

I chuckled and said, "You always were a wit."

Cal looked at me mystified.

"Forget it," I said.

Cal shrugged and said, "Tell me, Will, are Rabelais's books still in print?"

"Sure," I said, reaching to the shelf behind me. "I can lend you my Viking edition of *Gargantua and Pantagruel*."

"Good. That'll save me a trip back in time." He stuffed the book into the secret pouch of his cape. "Thanks, Will," he said. Then he added, "I'll tell you what. It's such a nice evening, why don't I go get Pepper and you get a girl and we'll all go out to dinner together?"

"That would be great," I said. "But…er…I'm afraid I don't have any prospects lined up."

Cal's brow furrowed with concern. He said, "Come on, Will. You don't mean to tell me there isn't a single girl you can ask out?"

"Single *or* married," I quipped, even as I fidgeted uncomfortably. "We all fall upon hard times, Cal. Metaphorically speaking, I've undergone a loss of my romantic powers similar to the loss of Splendid Powers you suffer under an argon-free atmosphere."

"Will, you don't mean you're…" He drew up short, unable to finish the sentence.

It took me a minute, but I finally got it. "Oh, no!" I blurted out. "I didn't mean anything like that. I've been considered pretty splendid once or twice myself, you know. What I meant to say is that I've lost the ability to get to know girls, let alone romance them."

"I know," Cal said. "How about if I bring my old boyhood friend Patti Pert along?"

The thought of going out with that fiery redhead made my head spin. But then I realized that it could never work out with Pepper and Patti at the same table. First thing you know, they'd be scheming to uncover Splendid Man's secret identity.

"I'm not sure that would be wise," I said.

"Isn't there any woman who interests you?"

"Well, there is a girl up the street I'm rather taken with."

"Well, there you are!" said Cal, clasping my shoulder. "Ask her if she's busy tonight."

"There's a problem with that. You see, I don't really know her very well."

"How well do you know her?"

"I usually see her when I go to Albertson's. I guess we keep similar schedules."

Splendid Man's brow furrowed. "Have you ever talked to her?"

"Once, when we were in the produce section together, I asked her if she knew how to select a good avocado."

"What did she say?"

"She doesn't speak English very well," I confessed.

"Where is she from?"

"I'm pretty sure she's Japanese."

Cal chuckled. "You know, it's funny. I've never been able to tell Japanese from Chinese. I guess it comes with being from another planet. But we should do something about this young lady you've been admiring from afar. If you know a little bit about her schedule, I think we could manage to have you encounter her."

"Well, I have happened to notice that she walks home from the bus stop at about 6:45 every evening, except every other Friday," I said. "But I'm afraid I won't be a very entertaining date if I can't speak her language."

"Don't worry about a thing, Will. With my power of Splendid Ventriloquism and my command of over six thousand Earth languages, including Japanese, I'll take care of everything. Fortunately, Pepper is in town on a newspaper assignment with my secret identity, Ken Clayton." Splendid Man had gotten into the habit of beginning every visit by sweeping my apartment for hidden microphones with his Splendid Senses, so he felt safe mentioning his various names. "I'll be back, as Ken, within a half hour." He opened the window and prepared to go.

"Cal?" I said.

"Yes, Will?" he said.

"Thanks," I said.

"Anything for a pal," he said. He waved and disappeared in a flash of red and gold.

Getting through the next half hour was hell. I changed clothes three times. I brushed my teeth twice. I even trimmed my beard. Was I really about to meet this woman who'd tantalized me so much from a distance? I tried to think of ways I could repay Splendid Man for making it possible. How could even the finest literary education possibly equal this? Not that the first and greatest of Splendid Heroes would ever expect repayment for anything he did for me or the rest of the human race, but still…

The doorbell rang and I jumped. It was 6:40. I greeted Cal in his guise as blue-suited reporter Ken Clayton. He introduced me to his companion, a perky brunette in a tailored yellow dress and a pillbox hat that managed at once to evoke the '60s and yet look utterly modern. They both seemed a little ill at ease, as if they'd just broken off an argument.

"Will Jones, this is my fellow reporter, Pepper Pine."

"Pleased to meet you, Will," said Pepper. "Ken tells me you're an aspiring writer."

"Well," I said awkwardly. "I do like to write."

Pepper chattered on. "I hope we aren't too early. Ken is always so nervous about being late. As you probably know, he doesn't exactly have nerves of steel."

Ken winked at me.

"We all have our faults," I said, smiling knowingly. "Would you like to come in for a drink?"

Pepper was about to accept, but Ken said suddenly, "I think it's time to go to dinner." His eyes were fixed at a spot on my wall, and I knew he was using the X-ray setting of his Splendid Vision to keep track of my Japanese woman.

"Honestly, Ken, you are the most nervous man I have ever known," said Pepper.

Just as Ken must have planned it, we saw the girl approaching when we reached the street. Suddenly, as we drew near, a pure white dog charged at her from nowhere, barking and snarling and foaming at the mouth. She screamed in horror. At that instant a blast of Ken's Splendid Breath picked me up and hurled me toward the dog. Not knowing what else to do, I yelled, "Scram! Scoot! Get out of here!" and waved my arms frantically.

The dog turned tail and ran. The woman nearly fainted, and I caught her in my arms. When the dog was far down the block it stopped, turned, winked at me, and flew into the air like a bullet. Only then did I realize it was Stronto, the loyal Splendid Dog of Splendid Man's boyhood, no doubt following its master's ultrasonic commands. Evidently, Ken was planning to make me the hero of the evening, without once revealing himself as the Man of Splendor.

When the Japanese girl regained her composure, and I had

reluctantly released her, I heard Ken whisper, "Bow, Will," above the pounding of my heart. As I did so, I heard strange Oriental words coming from my direction in a voice uncannily like my own. Good old Ken. The girl was soon chattering animatedly and I, still facing downward, was conversing with her. Suddenly she ran indoors.

"Why that's marvelous, Will!" bubbled Pepper. "How did you ever become so fluent in Chinese?"

"Well, actually, it's Japanese," I said. "And it isn't so difficult. The only tough part is learning to read from top to bottom."

Ken ventriloquized in a whisper to me, "Her name is Michiko, she's single, she's grateful, and she'll be right out. Remember, try to cover your mouth discreetly with a drinking glass or napkin whenever I speak Japanese for you."

With Michiko at my side we were soon en route to a local Japanese restaurant. At Pepper's insistence we sat at the sushi bar and sampled odd, nameless meats on rice balls.

"My, this is interesting food," said Pepper. "I hope we get some raw fish. We don't have things like this in Municipalitus. San Francisco is so colorful! Did Ken tell you why we're out here? We're doing a story on the gay singles scene for our Lifestyle section."

"That's fascinating," I said.

"I'll say," Pepper said. "In fact, it's finally opened my eyes."

"Now, Pepper," Ken said. "Don't start in on that again."

"Don't you 'now Pepper' me, Ken Clayton!" she snapped. "You know darn well I'm onto something here." She whirled on me and demanded, "Hasn't it ever occurred to you that Splendid Man is gay?"

I blinked. Then my jaw fell open. Then I threw back my head and laughed. "Is this a joke?" I sputtered.

"Look at me," Pepper said, without batting an eye. "Do you find me physically repulsive?"

"No!" I said. "On the contrary."

"Does it seem reasonable to you that a man would date me for years and never make a pass?"

"Now, Pepper," Ken broke in. "It's not nice to put Will on the spot."

Pepper started to retort, but broke off when Japanese sounds suddenly leapt from my direction. I quickly whipped my face in Michiko's direction and threw a sake cup before my lips to hide them. She looked a little perplexed, but whatever I said must have been witty, because she dropped her chopsticks to giggle behind her hand. She inclined her head toward me in laughter, her sable hair brushing my shoulder.

Pepper babbled on to Ken. It must have been a chore even for Splendid Man to keep up witty banter for me while not neglecting Pepper, but fortunately conversation with Pepper calls for less talking than listening. When he couldn't ventriloquize for me, he helped in other ways. A cool breeze sprang up and Michiko snuggled close to me for warmth. It was Ken with his Splendid Breath. When Michiko offered me a chunk of her raw fish and I wondered if I could summon up the courage to eat it, I noticed Ken discreetly cooking it with the heat setting of his Splendid Vision.

My only fear was that she would ask what I did for a living and Cal would give the wrong answer. After all, I was a novelist for life. I was only temporarily a fitting room supervisor at Mervyn's.

Suddenly I realized that Pepper was addressing me again. "Tell me, Will. Did you ever read the comic in which I was turned into Jungle Pepper?"

I nodded. "*Splendid Man's Paramour Pepper Pine*, issue 19."

"Well, if you think the artist made me look sexy, you should have seen me in real life. That leopard-skin shift was like a *USA Today* story—it barely covered the essentials, if you know what I mean. And what did Splendid Man do when he rescued me? He bundled me up in his cape!"

I couldn't believe my ears. I'd thought she'd been joking earlier. And yet she forged on, with no punchline in sight. "Then there was the time I adopted the role of Gun Moll Pepper to get the goods on a gangster. And was I one sweet dish! Eight-inch heels. Sheer black dress. Décolletage down to my navel. Lock of raven hair falling seductively over my left eye. And what did Mr.

Splendid say when he showed up to make the arrest? He told me I looked like Morticia Addams!"

Pepper smacked the tabletop with the palm of her hand. "Oh, and it isn't just me who leaves him cold! Take Ms. Torrid Redhead, Patti Pert. She mooned over him all those years when they were growing up together in Turnipville, and he never even tried to get to second base with her. This is a *teenage boy* I'm talking about. And her with those spandex sweaters! And Pura Poseidonis, the fish girl. Not that I can figure out how you're supposed to make it with a mermaid, but the point is that Splendid Fella never tried. You tell me, Will. What does all this add up to?"

"That he's not just the greatest hero in the universe, but the greatest gentleman as well," I said without missing a beat. Although I must admit that for a moment my words gave me pause. Could Splendid Man have carried his gallantry so far that he was still a virgin?

"Oh, I'll grant you that he's a gentleman," Pepper said. "But even a gentleman gives a girl a meaningful glance every decade or so. Look at you. You only just met your Vietnamese girl and already you're desperate to jump her skinny bones. Like a normal man!"

"Well, I do like to think I'm..." I started to say, but this time it was Ken who interrupted me.

"Tell me, Pepper," he said. "Do you think *I'm* gay?"

Pepper turned to him in surprise. And suddenly Japanese sounds were filling the air again, and I was fumbling for my bowl of miso soup. Good old Splendid Man. Even while having to listen to Pepper's nonsense, he was making sure I didn't lose any points with Michiko.

"Why in heaven's name would I think that?" I heard Pepper say over Michiko's titters.

"Well, since you've often suspected me of being Splendid Man," Ken said, "then it only stands to reason that...."

"Don't be ridiculous, Ken," Pepper said. But then her eyes were narrowing. "Wait a minute. *You've* dated me for years, too. And you've never made a pass at me either. Not even the time I posed as Nurse Pepper to get the lowdown on a twisted gynecologist, and even that two-sizes-too-small nurse's uniform couldn't get a rise out of you!" She broke off and her eyes opened wide. "But if you were secretly Splendid Man...!"

Ken chuckled. "Good old Pepper," he said. "You'll just never get that silly suspicion out of your head, will you?"

"Hey, no you don't," said Pepper. "No changing the subject. This isn't about Splendid Man's secret identity. It's about his secret orientation!" But Ken was sitting stock still, as if listening to something none of the rest of us could hear. "Excuse me, folks," he said, sauntering toward the restroom.

"Where do you think you're going?" Pepper called, but he just kept on walking.

Michiko looked at me, smiling expectantly. Her cheeks were flushed from drinking sake and her luxurious hair fell across one eye. The right eye, in this case. She made me forget Pepper's babblings in an instant. But I had no idea what to say. I tried to think of an intelligent question.

"Er...what did you think of Mishima's suicide?" I asked.

"I sorry," she said. "Japanese please."

I was saved from great embarrassment by sudden cries of "Splendid Man! Splendid Man!" from the tables by the windows. Apparently, his red and gold form had cloven the sky for an instant, and everyone was craning to see. Michiko ran to the windows.

Pepper jerked upright in the seat beside me. She stared misty-eyed toward the windows, a hand held to her throat. "What a man," I heard her sigh. "What a dreamboat. How could he possibly be...? How could I have ever doubted his...? Oh, what gets into me, anyway?!" But an instant later she was leaning toward me and whispering confidentially, "Have you ever noticed that Ken is never around when Splendid Man appears?"

I shrugged. "I'm sure it's just a coincidence."

"That's what Catman always says," she snapped. "I think you're all trying to keep something from me."

And just like that she seemed to be her old spunky self again. I guess years of unrequited love can cause some wild mood swings.

"Say, how did you and Ken meet, anyway?" she asked.

I gulped. I couldn't very well tell her that I'd known him as Splendid Man long before he'd "introduced" me to his mild-mannered alter ego.

"Well...er..." I said instead. "I went to Municipalitus for the...er...vintage paperback show and...er...Ken was covering it for your paper and we discovered that we both had a soft spot for the novels of...er...Jim Thompson."

"Well, look who's back, right on cue," she said, and I realized she hadn't been listening to a word I'd said. I turned to see Ken strolling back from the restroom, combing back his hair.

"What's all the excitement?" he asked. "Did I miss something?"

"You don't know a thing about it, I suppose?" said Pepper icily.

When Michiko returned, she squeezed my hand and bubbled over with words, probably about Splendid Man. I longed to say anything that would encourage her to keep seeing me. I figured that once Ken got her interested in me I could learn Japanese and keep things going on my own. Almost inaudibly I whispered, "Tell her that I can introduce her to Splendid Man." I knew only Ken's Splendid Hearing would pick up my words.

I cleverly arranged my chopsticks over my mouth and Ken promptly ventriloquized. Michiko looked perplexed. Ken tried again. The words were strange, full of P sounds and strongly rolled R's. Michiko asked a question in Japanese and this odd but vaguely familiar language filled the air more and more stridently. People turned around to stare. Then Ken gave up. Michiko drew away from me, troubled. I desperately tried to communicate with her.

"Er...you likee sushi?" I asked.

Suddenly she bolted from the sushi bar, tears shining in her eyes.

"You men!" Pepper cried. "Whatever did you say to that girl?" She ran after her to the bathroom.

I was dumbfounded. I shook Ken by the arm. "What happened? What was that language?"

"I don't understand it," he said. "I tried to speak Japanese and instead spoke Strontiumese, the language of my native planet Strontium on which all life was destroyed by a great flood when I was an infant. Then I tried Korean, Mandarin, and two of the Ainu dialects of Hokkaido, but for some reason whenever I try to speak a foreign language it comes out Strontiumese!"

"You were doing fine before you disappeared!"

"I picked up an ultrasonic intergalactic distress call with my Splendid Hearing," he said. "A planet of peaceful alien creatures orbiting Arcturus was being attacked by my old enemies in the Vengeance Is Mine Squad. I flew out to set things right and hurried back by the shortest—Great Amundsen! Now I remember! That lavender meteor I passed must have been composed of lavender strontiumite, the mysterious substance from the planet Strontium which mutates all Strontiumese natives in the most fantastic ways possible for forty-eight hours!"

"Damn it, Ken!" I snapped. "Forty-eight hours is too long! This is my only chance with Michiko, and she must already think I'm mocking her!"

I was frantic, but Ken, as always, remained calm. "You know, Will," he said, "lavender strontiumite always lands me in some seemingly inextricable predicament. But somehow a way out usually presents itself."

I fumed. "What is it with strontiumite, anyway? I mean, why the hell are there fragments of your planet floating around? Strontium was devastated by a *flood*. It's not like internal stresses made it explode or anything."

"That's true, Will. But the waves of the great flood were so powerful that they actually flung chunks of strontiumite into the air at such speed that they escaped the planet's gravitational pull and flew into outer space, where cosmic rays then transmuted them in various peculiar ways. Many of them hurtled to Earth as meteorites, while others, like the one I encountered this evening, continue to drift endlessly through space."

"Just my damned luck," I muttered.

"I'll admit that this is awfully bad timing. I'll have to think hard to get us out of this one."

"Well, you'd better think fast," I said. "Because here come the ladies."

Pepper approached us huffily while Michiko waited behind her, eyes averted. "I don't know what your friend said, Ken, but Mariko here thinks he doesn't want to talk to her anymore. I'm taking her home."

"Er…" I said.

"Now Pepper, I'm sure…er…Will didn't mean to offend her," said Ken.

Pepper angrily led Michiko to the door. Michiko turned to me with a look of sadness that tore my heart out. "Sayonara," she said.

"That means…" Ken started to say.

"I know," I interrupted. "Sayonara means goodbye."

But they never got to the door. To everyone's amazement, most of all mine, Splendid Man appeared. He strode through the restaurant, meeting the awed whispers of the patrons with a reassuring smile.

But wait a minute, you say! How can Splendid Man be here when his alter ego Ken Clayton is standing by my side? Can it be one of the Splendid Man robots Ken keeps in his Municipalitus apartment to help preserve his secret identity?

This Splendid Man, however, bowed to Michiko and addressed her in fluent Japanese. Michiko squealed and clapped her hands like a child. When Splendid Man finished his speech she turned to me and shook my hand.

"I sorry. Before I not understand what happen," she said. "I hope you feel better soon."

Mystified, I bowed and thanked her.

"Well," said Ken, "shall we finish our sushi?"

But Michiko, having said her piece to me, turned back to Splendid Man. He tried to extricate himself, but Michiko sidled close and pelted him with questions.

Ken frowned. I guess he could tell as well as I could that, despite all his trouble, Michiko wouldn't be thinking much of me anymore that night. "I'm sorry, Will," he said.

"I guess it just wasn't meant to be," I said.

Without moving his lips, Splendid Man suddenly said in English, "Pepper, this girl has had a trying night. Why don't you walk her home? I'll explain the whole situation to Ken and he can fill you in later."

"Well, all right," said Pepper reluctantly. She was gazing at Splendid Man with such naked longing that I could tell all the ridiculous accusations she'd made earlier were forgotten. "Come on, Yoko. If the men want to have secrets from us, let them." As they left, Michiko waved plaintively to Splendid Man alone, and Pepper muttered, "I was *sure* Ken was Splendid Man this time."

Outside, in the welcome darkness, Ken and Splendid Man and I found one of Splendid Man's robots waiting patiently.

"I want to get to the bottom of this mystery," I said. "Obviously, no robot could speak Japanese fluently without the aid of Splendid Ventriloquism. But, just like in the comics, one of your prominent friends could have disguised himself to resemble you and done your talking for you."

"Yes," said Ken. "By sending a whispered command ultrasonically to Municipalitus, I ordered this robot to find a Japanese-speaking friend and whisk him here, along with a Splendid Disguise kit. Then I informed my friend of the problem in English by Splendid Ventriloquism, and he was able to save both the social situation and my secret identity."

"Let me guess," I said, gesturing toward the ersatz Splendid Man. "Under that lifelike rubber mask is the face of Wyatt Brewster, better know as Catman!"

"That's a good guess," said Ken. "But even the remarkably well-educated Wyatt Brewster isn't fully conversant in the Asian languages. For this delicate assignment I needed someone in complete command of Japanese."

The false Splendid Man peeled the rubber mask from his head to reveal the face of an ancient Asian man in spectacles.

"Will, this is my friend Hirohito, the Emperor of Japan," said Ken. "Your Excellency, this is my friend Will Jones."

"Well, this is a surprise," I said.

"Very pleased to meet you," said Emperor Hirohito in accented but elegant English. "Splendid Man inform me that you wish to be novelist."

"Well," I admitted, "I do like to write. But tell me, what did you say to Michiko?"

"Ah, very simple," said the Emperor with a quick bow. "This one say to young lady that Splendid Man battle old nemesis, evil genius Pox Pascal, in sky above San Francisco. During this battle, malevolent ray from Pascal's villainous device strike unfortunate Jones-san, making him unable to speak our humble Japanese language."

"It's awfully nice of you to go out of your way to help me," I said.

"Hirohito and I became rather close a few years ago when I stopped a radioactive, fire-breathing dinosaur from destroying Tokyo," said Ken, putting his arm around the elderly nobleman. "But now I guess I should have my robot whisk him back to the Imperial Palace in Tokyo before he's missed."

"Please, one moment," said the Emperor. He backed away, fishing in the pouch of his Splendid Man uniform. "Please stand together," he said, drawing out a Nikon camera with a flash attachment.

Ken and I posed, Hirohito snapped a picture, then Hirohito and Ken posed, and then the Emperor and I. At last we bowed and shook hands.

"This one hope to meet you again, Jones-san," said the Emperor. "And please, visit me anytime, Splendid Man. I mean…Clayton-san!" He giggled and replaced the rubber mask of Splendid Man. The Splendid Robot gathered him up, wrapped him in its cape to shield him from the buffeting of the wind on his trans-Pacific flight, and launched itself into the sky. We waved until they were out of sight.

"Cup of coffee?" asked Ken as we walked along the dark

street, watching the fog pour in from the ocean.

"Maybe you should get back to Pepper," I said.

"Please don't think harshly of Pepper," Ken said. "She gets a little frustrated sometimes, but she's really a lovely person."

"Of course she is," I said.

"And sometimes she says things that are…well…better left unsaid."

As miserable as I was, that got a laugh out of me. "She sure has a wild imagination," I said. "Who could possibly think that Splendid Man is gay?"

Ken didn't laugh. He seemed lost in thought, and we walked silently for a while. At length he said, "Will?"

"What, Cal?"

He seemed oddly hesitant when he said, "Will…I think you should know…"

"What is it, pal?"

Then he sighed. "I think you should know how sorry I am about the way things turned out tonight," he said. "Lavender strontiumite always picks the worst times to afflict me. I should have been more careful."

"Don't worry about it," I said. "I've learned a lesson from tonight. Nobody can make me more appealing to a woman than I already am, not even Splendid Man."

"There are a million fish in the sea, Will," said Ken.

"She seemed taken with you," I said. "Or at least with Emperor Hirohito dressed up as you. Will you be seeing her yourself?"

"I wouldn't do that to you, Will," said Ken. "Neither would Hirohito. You know, a lot of fellows who were raised to believe they were the direct descendant of the Sun Goddess and then suddenly had to get used to being just another guy might go around with a chip on their shoulder. But he's as decent as they come."

"At least I can feel that Michiko doesn't hate me," I said. "Though I guess I'll never be able to see her again."

We stood on a hill looking out at the lights of the city, softened by the fog. Ken put his arm around me.

"I know it's disappointing, Will," he said. "But think of the heartwarming lesson we've learned. You may have lost a girl, but we've seen how the leaders of the free nations of the world can come to the aid of their allies in solving international problems."

"Yes," I said. "That's some consolation."

Episode Four
Splendid Man: The Movie

We had to stand in line for two hours to get into the movie. I considered asking Ken to sneak us in at Splendid Speed, but I knew he would never use his powers for his own advantage.

The movie wasn't worth the wait. It was long on violence and special effects, short on character and verisimilitude. And it portrayed the hero as tough and vengeful, rather than noble and just. I felt Ken squirm beside me several times and suspected he felt as did I. The crowd seemed to love it, though. I guess there's no accounting for taste.

The only good thing about the movie was Lance DeWilde, the unknown actor who had been cast to portray the Man of Splendor. I reflected on the irony that his name was so reminiscent of Tyrone DeBold's, the actor who had played Splendid Man in the TV show all those years ago. But where DeBold had been broad of frame and rather craggy of feature, this new kid very nearly mirrored Splendid Man's panther-like grace and classic good looks. Not to mention how uncannily he captured the vaguely effeminate air Splendid Man assumes in his secret identity of Ken Clayton.

Ken seemed pensive when we left the theater. I was about to ask what was the matter when a young autograph hound ran up crying, "Hey! Aren't you Lance DeWilde?"

Ken simply said, "No." I had never seen him so curt with anyone before.

A few blocks later, after the crowd had thinned out, we were finally able to talk.

"I'm not like that, am I, Will?" he asked.

"Don't be silly," I said. "It's only a movie. You know what a lousy job Hollywood does when they base a movie on a real person. Look at *Caligula.*"

"A bad story I could stand. It's the way they portrayed me. Tell me, Will, do you think I'd stoop to beating the bad guy insensate? Do you think I'd take personal retribution on some poor twisted soul who felt a life of crime was his only recourse?"

"But that's how so many Splendid Heroes are portrayed these days. Look at what they did to Catman in his movie. We both know he would never douse a villain with gasoline and set him on fire."

"I can't believe the way the audience reacted," he went on, as if he hadn't heard a word I'd said. "Is that what people want from me? Do they want the self-appointed guardian of mankind to use his Splendid Powers to vindicate himself on personal enemies?"

I'd never seen Splendid Man so upset, not even when he'd told me of how he had been unwittingly responsible for the deaths of his foster parents, Joseph and Mary Clayton, when he'd taken them vacationing to a deserted Pacific atoll having forgotten that it was to be the site of an atomic bomb test.

"And another thing," Ken said. "Do they take my vow to mankind so lightly? Do they think I'd give up my Splendid Powers just for the love of a woman? Tell me, Will. Would you marry a woman who demanded that you give up writing?"

"Well…"

"I thought not. I'm very fond of Pepper, Will. Have no doubt about it. But what makes these filmmakers think that after years of dating I would suddenly give up everything for her hand in marriage? Do they think that after decades of preserving my secret identity through innumerable clever ruses, I would give it away by absentmindedly sticking my hand in a meat grinder? And besides, is it fair to Pepper? It's just going to get her hopes up again, and you don't know how it distresses me to see her get hurt."

"Maybe you should view the movie as an imaginary story, such as the comics used to feature," I suggested. "Like the one in which Pepper is rocketed to Strontium as a tot and becomes the Splendid Woman from Earth. Or the one in which you're injected with a serum as an infant which causes you to grow into the High Rise

Splendid Boy. Or the one…"

"You know as well as I do that comic book sales are down, Will. Millions of people out there will see this movie and take that picture of me for what I really am, instead of the picture my pals at AC/DC Comics have been faithfully painting of me for all these years. That guy who wrote the movie, that Jerry Jacobs, he'd really be in trouble if I were the kind of guy he made me out to be. I'd fly down to Hollywood this minute and let him have it. Pow! Right in the kisser!"

We came upon a cafe that was open late. When I suggested that we get a cup of coffee, Ken followed me silently. It was one of those places that tries for an old-fashioned decor. It even had a revolving door.

Ken brooded silently at the table. I tried to cheer him up. "Think of it this way," I said. "Sure, the movie showed you being petty and thuggish. It shouldn't have. But at least it showed good triumphing over evil."

"Did it, Will?" When the coffee came, Ken sipped at his listlessly. He looked so depressed, I wondered if there might not be some silver strontiumite secreted nearby. "Did it show good triumphing over evil? It showed a hero, who is supposed to represent good, giving in to all sorts of self-indulgences. Of course, everybody is tempted by revenge and sex and cutting into a long line. But part of standing up for goodness is resisting those temptations, doing what's best for mankind."

"That's true," I said. "But a lot of teenage moviegoers would have trouble identifying with that."

"That's the trouble with this world!" yelled Ken, pounding his fist on the table. People stared. Fortunately, even in his anger, he held back his Splendid Strength, and the table wasn't reduced to sawdust. "Why can't youngsters identify with someone who commits himself to the good of other people? When I was a boy, growing up in Turnipville, my friends and I thought of nothing but what was right. If it ever appeared that my parents or my boyhood friends Roswell Smutts or Patti Pert or my loyal Splendid Dog Stronto had done some wrong, it was invariably either a misunderstanding or the scheme of some dastardly villain!"

When he finished his tirade, the cloud came back into his eyes. "I don't know," he said, stirring his coffee idly. "The world was simpler then. Maybe I'm just out of date."

"But you continue to be the idol of billions," I said. "You've inspired generations with your never-ending battle for truth, justice, and the democratic, humanist way. The good people of Earth can sleep secure in their beds, knowing that you are watching over them."

"Don't try to cheer me up, Will," he sighed. "I know how helpless I am. What can my Splendid Strength do against drug abuse? What can all the settings of my Splendid Vision do against rampant teenage sexual promiscuity? What can Splendid Speed do to quell alcoholism in the home? How can Splendid Breath prevent the breakdown of the American family? How can Splendid Ventriloquism relieve hunger in the third world? Can even my Strontiumese invulnerability turn back the rising tide of homophobia?" He shook his head dismally.

Somehow I had to bring my pal out of his profound depression. I thought I'd been glum over my financial and romantic problems, but now I realized what a burden the hero of heroes must bear on his mighty shoulders. Even the worst days at my temporary telemarketing job couldn't compare to this. I felt a little selfish.

"I've never heard you like this before," I said.

"I try not to show it," he said. "It would dispirit too many people. You know, I've always had the feeling that my Splendid-Powered pals in the North American Alliance for Meetness look up to me, and I know I'm a big influence on my little cousin Splendid Girl and such other young heroes as the Array of Splendid Striplings and the Pubescent Paladins, that posse of powerful sidekicks. What would they all think if Splendid Man sat around crying into his coffee instead of taking action?"

"Do you feel like this a lot?"

"When something happens to me to make me feel helpless," he said. "The only way to fight the feeling is to fly. It's like that book you gave me for my last birthday, *Zorba the Greek*. Zorba dances,

I fly. When Ma and Pa Clayton were vaporized by that atomic blast, I flew. When I first failed to free the Strontiumese city of Strontor from the can into which the blue android space criminal Cerebriac had shrunk it, I flew. I know what the Strontorians thought: That Splendid Man, he is a madman! Here we are, shrunk into a can, and he flies! But if I did not fly I would burst with grief. No one, my friend, not even a native of Strontium under the influence of Earth's argon-tinged atmosphere and lesser gravity, is invulnerable to a broken heart. When I look over the earth and see how miserable people are and how little Splendid Man can do for them, then I have to fly. I have to fight malevolent villains! I have to smash runaway planetoids!'"

"But you do good," I said. "What if you weren't there to perform urgent missions in outer space? What if you didn't fight Cerebriac, and San Francisco got shrunk into a can of Manwich? Think how much misery there would be."

Ken lowered his head despondently. "I try," he said. "But then this movie comes along. It makes me wonder about the whole thing."

Just then, an aging autograph hunter came to the table, calling, "Hey, aren't you Tyrone DeBold? I thought you'd jumped off a bridge."

For a moment, I thought Ken was going to vindicate the moviemakers and hit him. Then he grabbed the man's autograph book, scribbled something quickly, and shoved it back at him. The man read it, said, "Asshole," and walked away.

"How did you sign it?" I asked.

"Soupy Sales," he said.

I could see he was becoming bad-tempered. "Listen, what you need is a drink. It'll take your mind off it."

"Drinking won't help, Will. With my invulnerable brain cells, alcohol has no effect on my mood or behavior. As much as I enjoy the taste and social ritual of liquor, I could never get drunk except under an argon-free atmosphere."

I shook my head. "I guess invulnerability isn't everything."

Abruptly he stood up, staring off into space. "Excuse me,

Will," he said, and hurried to the revolving door. He spun himself around the door so fast that he and it became a blur. Out flew Splendid Man, where Ken Clayton had been mere moments before. The revolving door slowly rotated to a stop.

I waited quite a while for him to return, long enough to finish my coffee. At last I got up and went to the men's room. When I returned, Ken was waiting for me at the table. He looked refreshed.

"What happened?" I asked.

"Giganto the Splendid Mandrill escaped from the distant past in which I had imprisoned him," he said. "He was wreaking havoc in Municipalitus, seeking vengeance on me, the little red and gold man who originally captured him. Defeating him wasn't easy, but I had virtue on my side."

"There, you see," I said. "How many people would have been hurt if you hadn't been here?"

"It wasn't like that movie, I'll tell you," he said. "The villain in the movie hit Splendid Man with a nuclear sub and he vanished for twenty minutes before he came crawling back like some ninety-seven pound weakling. But not me! I've been hit with much bigger things than nuclear subs in my time, and I'm none the worse for it. I'd like to see that Hollywood Splendid Man tangle with a giant mandrill with strontiumite eyes!"

I could see that the change of pace had perked him up. I said, "Let's pay the check and go out for a while. Maybe we could fly somewhere."

He caught my wrist. "Tell me, Will. Tell me the truth. I do help people, don't I?"

"Yes, you do, Ken."

"And you believe I do it for the good of mankind, don't you?"

"Of course I do. We all do."

"And I'm not like that Splendid Man in the movie, am I?"

"Not a bit."

"One more thing, Will. Do I really look like Lance DeWilde? I mean, I always gave myself some credit for having character in my face. I'm not really that boyishly cute, am I?"

"Well...er...don't worry about that," I said. "After all,

DeWilde's just a movie star. You're the Man of Splendor. He can't even fly without machines."

"I suppose not," said Ken. "But you know, once or twice in the movie I almost believed he could. It's too bad they can't use all that money and all those special effects to make a good movie."

"Well," I said, "that's Hollywood."

"Yes, and I guess that's life," he said, and we left the cafe much happier than when we'd entered it.

Episode Five
Literary Lad

I was working on a new story when Splendid Man called from the Gobi Desert to ask if he could drop by for a visit. Actually, he hadn't literally "called," but contacted me using his Splendid Directional Voice Casting. I faced southeast and nodded, knowing he'd see my response with the telescopic setting of his Splendid Vision. A moment later he wafted through an open window into my apartment.

"Hi, pal," he said.

"Hi, pal," I said.

"Did I interrupt anything?"

"Oh no, I was only writing," I said.

"Can I read it?" he asked.

"Well, it's not finished yet," I said. He looked hurt, so I added hastily, "I would like your opinion, though. After all, you're getting to be quite knowledgeable about literature."

"Thanks, Will," he said, going to my desk. "By the way, I really enjoyed *The Sun Also Rises*."

"Great. What did you think of the scene where Jake and Bill go fishing in the mountains? Wasn't Hemingway's description of the wine being so cold that it hurt the backs of their eyes just great?"

"I wouldn't know anything about pain," he mumbled. I could tell he was already absorbed in my story.

I lit a cigarette and paced nervously, waiting for his judgment. Of course, I knew that his opinion wouldn't really matter, since not even Splendid Man could be objective about a story based on himself.

"This is terrific, Will," he finally said. "It reminds me of Northern Light's Casebook, in which Fugface, his Siberian grease monkey, records all of his colorful adventures."

"Yes," I said. "It is very much like that, only different."

"Not that I would call this story particularly colorful. Boy, I really let that movie get me down, didn't I? You certainly describe it vividly, though. Your writing really seems to be coming along."

"I like to think so, Cal," I said morosely. "But what's the point of it all, really? Will people remember me a thousand years from now?"

"Why, I don't know, Will," he said. "But shouldn't you worry about getting published first?"

"Sure," I said. "There's that. But every artist dreams of immortality for his works and fears the thought of someday being forgotten. I know you understand, Cal. You're always present at the ceremonial unveilings of the many statues and monuments erected in your honor throughout the universe."

He looked thoughtful and absentmindedly fumbled for a cigarette in the pack I'd left on the desk. "Is this really weighing on you, Will?"

I shrugged. "Maybe it's just my temporary job sticking those little labels on tomatoes that's getting me down. But no, there's more to it than that. I've been feeling blue ever since I read the *Iliad*. I was awed that any book could survive for so many centuries—and then it hit me that my books might be forgotten mere decades after my death. Sure, I could be like Stephen King and make a million dollars on some ephemeral trash. But who's going to remember *The Stand* or *Carrie* a hundred years from now, let alone a thousand? Hell, who remembers *Cujo* today?"

"Wasn't that the one about the malevolent dog?" asked Cal.

"Okay, *you* remember," I said. "But that's only because you have the power of Splendid Recall. By the time you and I are gone, *Cujo* may as well never have existed—a fate I wouldn't wish on a malevolent dog! How do I know my work isn't going to suffer the same oblivion?"

Cal mulled over my words for a few moments, puffing on the cigarette, and said, "There's only one way we can find out for sure."

"How's that?" I asked.

"Simple. We can take a little trip into the future."

"No kidding?" I exclaimed.

"Now that I think about it," he said, "I haven't visited my young friends in the Array of Splendid Striplings for quite some time. We can kill two birds with one stone. Figuratively speaking, of course, as my code prevents the taking of all life."

"Great!" I said. "The Array of Splendid Striplings!"

Without further ado, Cal bundled me in his cape, opened the window, and shot into the sky, instantly exceeding the speed of light. Braving mortal harm from the temporal winds that would have buffeted me to death if not for the indestructible cape that enfolded my body, I uncovered my eyes for a peak at the trans-temporal landscape. Sure enough, we were speeding through a tunnel of multicolored concentric rings, the dates posted between each ring in blurry black numerals. Within moments, we materialized in front of the Stripling clubhouse in the year 2982.

Maybe you're like me, and you've always wondered how the Stripling Clubhouse can be so vast indoors but appear so unimposing from the exterior. Believe me, this discrepancy is the fault of the comic book artists. The place is huge, easily dwarfing the Transamerica Pyramid.

As we landed on Stripling Plaza, a welcoming committee of Striplings emerged from the clubhouse. I saw Uranus Lass and Multi Girl. I saw Mesmer Miss and Kangaroo Kid and Cerebriac 6.2. They were all dressed in their colorful Stripling garb. I expected Splendid Man to introduce me, but before he had a chance to do so, the Striplings crowded around me, exclaiming in chorus, "It's the Bard! The Bard himself!"

I didn't know what they were talking about at first, until I noticed that they all carried books in their hands. Multi Girl was the first to shove hers at me, stammering, "M-m-may I have your autograph, M-M-Mr. Jones?"

My heart beat a tattoo against my chest as I took the book from her hands and saw, inscribed in bold red letters across the top, the name "Will C. Jones." But even more surprising was realizing that the title of the book was totally unfamiliar to me. Here I was, a thousand years in the future, about to autograph a book I hadn't even written yet!

When I took it from her and started to open it, she gasped, "J-j-just autograph the cover!"

"Okay," I said. "But I'd love to take a look at..."

"Er...there'll be plenty of time for that later," said Splendid Man. "Now let's have the Striplings give you a tour of their clubhouse. I'll tell you what, Will. I'll leave you here with the *teenage* Array of Splendid Striplings, who are better known to you from the comics, while I fly a little further into the future to visit my pals the Adult Striplings."

When I saw the way the girls were gazing at me, I hoped Splendid Man wouldn't hurry back. I hadn't had so many lovely young women adoring me like that since high school, and then I'd only been fantasizing.

Abruptly Kangaroo Kid, with his overdeveloped legs, bounced between me and the girls. He barked, "Here in the 30th Century, we consider you a literary immortal, Mr. Jones!"

"Well, I do like to think I'm ahead of my time," I said, reaching for the book in his hand. "But I'd love to take a look at..."

"Let's...er...give Mr. Jones that tour!" blurted Mesmer Miss, pulling me suddenly through the giant doors of the clubhouse.

It was killing me not being able to look in that book. What had I written about? Had I finally found my narrative voice? Had I learned to liven up my dialogue? And why would I have named it *Tender Is the August Light*? But the kids really seemed to have their hearts set on giving me this tour, and Will Jones was one literary immortal who was not going to disappoint his fans.

My tour guide was Cerebriac 6.2, the futuristic upgrade of that 20th Century Cerebriac whose faulty operating system had turned him into a notorious space criminal. "This is the Stripling lobby and reception area, Mr. Jones," he said, "housing a 30th Century Menti-Projector which beams a perpetual tape recounting the colorful origins of all the Striplings directly into the viewer's cerebral cortex, thus rendering vision unnecessary."

"That's very interesting," I said, as convincingly as I could.

From there we went up to Level 1, where Cerebriac 6.2 explained, "Here is where our arsenal and nuclear power generators, both powered by quintile crystals, are housed. To protect them, the walls of the Stripling Clubhouse are reinforced with magno-plastic lined with maxo-inertron, the most durable of all cosmic alloys. Needless to say, they are able to withstand the most powerful of attacks."

Cerebriac 6.2, with his Positronic Brain from the 8th Dimension, was as intelligent as I'd always heard. Unfortunately, too much brain can make you boring.

"So tell me," I said. "How many of my books are still in print here in the 30th Century?"

"Er...that sounds like a perfect question for The Marvelous Construct," he said, "that computational device so advanced that it can discover any information and fabricate any object known to sentient life. I shall be taking you to it soon."

"Swell," I said. "And do you know if they've been published on many other planets?"

"Since you bring up other planets," he said hastily, "I'm sure you will be fascinated by the Monitor Cubicle, where the progress of such other Striplings as Pig-Out Boy, the Too-Tall Kid, and Peanut can be followed in their various missions on color screens."

"Whatever," I said. "How about movies? Have any major motion pictures been based on my books? And have any biographies been written about me? How well did they capture the man...the artist?"

He opened his mouth, looking a little disconcerted, but before he could answer I was pelted by female voices:

"Where do you get your ideas?"

"Since all your books are set in the 20th Century, does that mean you write from life?"

"Did you grow your beard in honor of Hemingway or did he grow his in honor of you?"

I turned and found all three girls crowding up against me. No, make that all five girls—three of whom were physically identical. I was thrown for a moment, until I remembered Multi Girl's power of Splendid Self Duplication. All three of her were gazing up at me with big liquidy eyes.

"Did you choose literature or did it choose you?" asked one Multi Girl.

"Do you read reviews of your books?" asked another.

"Do you have to suffer to be an author?" asked the third.

"Well," I said, "hardship does help the author hone his vision." The Multi Girls sighed.

"Hey, Splendid Heroes have hardships too!" said Kangaroo Kid churlishly. "Multi Girl, remember the time I single-handedly defeated the piranha-birds of Alabaster VI? Or the time I saved the people of Diphthong II from a horde of two-legged spider beasts? Or the time I used my remarkable hopping ability to repel an invasion of Ganymedean brain suckers?"

The Multi Girls batted their eyes at me.

"How did it feel when you won your first Pulitzer?"

"Why do most authors commit suicide?"

"Is it true that authors drink and smoke a lot?"

"Well," I answered, "drinking and smoking do help the author hone his vision. Speaking of which, would you say my vision changed the direction of fiction in general? Did I inspire any literary movements? Did I ever appear on the Dick Cavett show?"

Abruptly, Kangaroo Kid, with his commodious limbs, launched into a series of hopping tricks such as no 20th Century acrobat could have imagined possible. "Remember this, Multi Girl?" he yelled. "Remember how I repelled the brain suckers? Look at me, Multi Girl! Look at me!"

The Multi Girls rolled all six of their eyes and said, "There seems to be some annoying noise around here. Let's go someplace quiet where we can talk about literature."

"Uh, sure," I said, as two Multi Girls each slipped an arm through mine and the third tugged me forward by my lapel. "And while we're at it, did I ever win the Nobel? Is there a plaque on my old apartment building in the Richmond District? Have any statues been erected in my honor? Did…"

The words died in my throat. Suddenly a fourth Multi Girl appeared before us, but where the others were Platonic ideals of youthful beauty, this was a parody of adolescence, all acne, braces, and greasy hair.

"You quit that, Mesmer Miss!" snarled the other three Multi Girls in chorus. "You're not going to make the Bard like you better with a stupid trick like that!"

The fourth Multi Girl dissolved into a golden cloud, and Mesmer Miss stepped through it, gazing worshipfully at me. "I just wanted the Bard to appreciate my Splendid Power of Illusion," she said, "so that it would mean more when I told him how amazed I was by the illusion of reality he cast in his novels with no Splendid Powers at all."

"Uh, thanks," I said. It was beginning to dawn on me that something odd was going on. You can't blame youngsters for going gaga over a literary immortal, but these gals were just a little too doe-eyed and dewy-lipped for comfort. And the racket of Kangaroo Kid bouncing frantically off the walls didn't exactly settle my nerves.

Mesmer Miss was getting a little too close to me when words filled my head. "Don't waste your time with these children, Mr. Jones. Or may I address you telepathically as Will?" That's when I noticed Uranus Lass smiling coyly at me. "I think you'll find that with my Splendid Mind Reading Power, I've developed an insight into the human soul quite advanced for my age. Of course, it's nothing compared to *yours*!"

Suddenly Mesmer Miss turned snarling on her teammate. "No fair, Uranus Lass! I know you're thinking to the Bard! No fair using Splendid Powers to get him all to yourself!"

"No fair, she says!" Uranus Lass telepathed. "It just so happens that she's using her Power of Illusion right now to hide a humongous zit on the tip of her nose!"

"You'd better not be telling him about my zit!" screeched Mesmer Miss.

"Just remember, Bard," thought Uranus Lass, "with me, what

you see is what you get—as Negroes used to say before the advancement of science rendered urban slang obsolete."

Cerebriac 6.2, with his Positronic Brain from the 8th Dimension, must have sensed the tension in the air, because he suddenly asked, "Mr. Jones, would you care to visit the room in which is housed The Marvelous Construct, which can grant any wish, no matter how subliminal, even if one were to wish unconsciously, for example, for the end of the universe, and is thus the most dangerous device in existence?"

But before the words were out of his mouth, the girls were going at each other, slapping, pulling hair, and kicking each other's ankles. I was appalled at the effect my fame was having on the integrity of those ordinarily self-sacrificing Splendid Heroines. Apparently even literary genius has its down side.

I had to get out of there. It was the decent thing to do, I knew, the only way I could restore peace and allow them to repair their friendships. Plus I didn't like the look in Kangaroo Kid's eyes as he came bouncing toward me.

"Take me to that Construct!" I yelled to Cerebriac 6.2.

But as I turned to run, something even stranger happened. Each of the Multi Girls split in two like an amoeba, and suddenly, while three duplicates kept up the fight with Uranus Lass and Mesmer Miss, three more were running full tilt at *me*.

"Don't worry, Bard!" one whispered.

"We'll ditch those hussies!" hissed another.

"From now on, it's just you and us!" whispered the third.

The three of them grabbed me and dragged me down the hall. They shoved me into a room and slammed the door behind me. I glanced around. I took in the canopy bed, the stuffed animals, the brightly hued cosmetics on the dresser, the lacy brassieres scattered on the floor, and the poster of what could only be a 30th Century teen heartthrob, and I realized to my horror that I was in a teenage girl's bedroom. And by the extraordinary number of mirrors lining the walls I realized it must be Multi Girl's.

"Now, wait a minute…" I began, hoping some authority was getting past the quaver in my voice.

"Please, Bard," said one of the Multi Girls. "Don't leave yet. I just want your autograph."

"Well, if that's all," I said with a sigh of relief, "I suppose I can..."

And suddenly all three of them were gripping the necklines of their bodysuits and starting to tug them lower. "In history class they told us how 20th Century groupies liked to have celebrities autograph their chests!" she giggled. "The other girls will turn green when they learn I've got the Bard's autograph on *all* my chests!"

"W-w-wait a minute!" I wailed, and tried to get around them to the door. But the Multi Girls did that amoeba thing again, and suddenly there were six teenage beauties barring my way, all stretching the fabric of their tops and about to expose an even dozen underage breasts. Visions of spending the rest of my life as the only literary immortal in a 30th Century maxo-inertron penitentiary began filling my mind.

"Do you have a Sharpie?" all six asked.

And then I was saved. The door flew open and the malformed figure of Kangaroo Kid exploded into the room. "All right, Multi Girl! Don't you think you're taking this a little too far? Just because we agreed to Splendid Man's scheme to trick Will into thinking that his books survived for a thousand years doesn't mean you have to throw yourselves all over him! We're supposed to be reinforcing his literary ambition, not his perversions!"

"Who are you to talk, you lop-eared freak?!" snapped one of the Multi Girls. "How many times have you asked all of me to..."

"What?" I said. They all stopped dead as I tried to find my voice. "Is this true? Has my pal Splendid Man deceived me?"

The other Striplings had crowded in behind Kangaroo Kid, but none seemed to have the nerve to speak. At last Uranus Girl telepathed to me, "I'm sorry, Mr. Jones, but I'm afraid it's true. Earlier, when Splendid Man said he was flying to the future to visit the Adult Striplings, he was really flying an hour into the past to tell us you were coming and set up his plan to boost your confidence. He made up a literary-sounding book title and then we used The Marvelous Construct to make fake covers and slap them on several copies of one of the classics in our library. Please don't hold it against us, Mr. Jones. We only did it so you'd go back to the 20th Century inspired to keep writing."

"We never expected that all of us girls would find you so, you know, *exciting*," said Mesmer Miss. "Especially considering that Multi Girl has been selected to mate with Kangaroo Kid, Uranus Lass has been matched with Sleet Lad, and I'm been designated a perfect partner for Shaolin Five Animals Kung-Fu Kid. It's just that we're not accustomed to meeting such...well... masculine men from the 20th Century."

"Not to mention that the advancement of science long ago rendered male sex appeal obsolete," added Multi Girl. "Our bodies just have no natural defenses against your pheromones!"

I was crushed. The other Striplings stared at their feet, saying nothing. Moments later, when Cerebriac 6.2, with his Positronic brain from the 8th Dimension, began to speak, I realized that they had all been conferring telepathically, linked by Uranus Lass's power.

"Despite this little hoax, Bar...er...Mr. Jones...and despite the fact that we were unable to find any of your works in the libraries of the seven hundred eighty-two planets which we scanned before you arrived here...we know you really are a good writer, because we've monitored your stories on our time screens. In fact, we all agree that your literary prowess is so impressive as to constitute a Splendid Power. Since this power with words is duplicated by no other Stripling and so does not violate our charter, and in spite of the fact that you are no longer a teenager, which manifestly does, we have elected you an honorary member of the Array of Splendid Striplings, along with Patti Pert in her role as Bug Babe, Bobby Anderssen because of the many times he's fought evil as Centipede Lad, and Splendid Man's boyhood pal, Roswell Smutts. I hereby christen you Literary Lad!"

"Gee, thanks," I said, somewhat heartened.

Just then, Splendid Man returned from his bogus mission into the future. I could tell from his averted glance that Uranus Lass had already informed him of the situation telepathically.

"Well, Will, I guess we should go home," he said quietly.

"We're really sorry, Will," said Kangaroo Kid remorsefully as Cal wrapped me in his cape.

"That's okay," I said. "I'll get over it. In time."

We flew along the time stream in silence. Splendid Man dropped me off at my apartment, mumbled an embarrassed goodbye, and disappeared into the sky. Only then did I pull from my coat the book I had swiped from the future. I allowed myself one last look at my name on the cover. Then I opened it to see what immortal literary classic it was that the young heroes of the future actually kept in their library. I flipped to a page at random and read: "The dog had shat on the garage floor. He had never known Cujo to do such a thing, not even as a pup."

Episode Six
Prisoner of Pox Pascal

Sometimes when my writing is going badly I like to torture myself by looking at the racks of paperback bestsellers. When I'm losing faith that I'll ever be able to write another decent paragraph, let alone get published, I can't resist the shot of envy and bitterness I get from scanning the glossy covers of all those Peter Benchley and Mario Puzo novels and thinking about the fortunes other writers have amassed by cleverly avoiding any sort of literary voice. Thus it was that I was striding into the foggy night toward my local 24-hour Walgreens, abandoning Chapter 68 of my latest novel about a man too passionate to fit into the everyday work world, eager to see what was new from Arthur Hailey or Michael Crichton or that literary immortal of the future, Stephen King.

So intent was I on my own misery that I nearly crashed into the man standing on the street corner. I jumped back and started to apologize. Then I noticed his eyebrows. Or, rather, his lack of same.

"Pox Pascal!" I gasped. "What do you want with me?"

"I want information that only you possess, Will Jones," sneered the criminal mastermind.

"I've got nothing to tell you," I said.

"I think I will be the judge of that, Will Jones."

"Judge away," I said. "But why do you think I'd cooperate with you?"

"I have monitored you with my hyperscientific devices for months," he said, "ever since you first became my enemy's pal, waiting for the inevitable day when the stars would fall from your eyes like meteors and you would begin to see the flaws in the friend you once venerated!"

"That's ridiculous," I said. "Yeah, sure, he got on my nerves a little with that fake book stunt he pulled. But there's no one who doesn't think Splendid Man is the greatest man in the world—and you're the most nefarious!"

"Really? What about every citizen of the planet Poxor, where I am revered as a hero and your Splendid Pal is despised as a villain?" He moved a hand slightly, and in the air beside me appeared a giant plastic sphere, as big as my bathroom and as transparent as a soap bubble. "Won't you join me on a trip to Poxor, Will Jones? It might…broaden your horizons."

My hand snaked to my pocket and vibrated the teeth of my SOS Comb. Let's see the grinning fiend act so superior when Splendid Man came to my rescue, I thought. Any second now, I thought. Okay, I thought. Any second…now?

"A problem?" Pascal smirked. "Is it your SOS Comb, perhaps, that isn't working?"

"You fiend," I snarled. "You've no doubt rigged up a jamming device."

"Yes," he chortled. "No doubt I have."

Before I knew what was happening, a hole had opened in the membrane of the bubble and Pascal had shoved me inside. I found myself standing on an invisible floor within the odd vessel. As I looked down through it, I saw the sidewalk receding beneath my feet. We were taking to the air! The rooftops and hills of San Francisco vanished as we gathered speed upward.

I took a hard look at my companion, then. The gleaming, hairless brows. The great crest of silver hair sweeping high above his head, as if to compensate for the naked forehead. The penetrating blue gems of his eyes and the lips twisted with lifelong bitterness. The lab smock he always wore in case anyone should fail to recognize him as a scientific genius. I realized then what it was that this arrogant scoundrel must want from me, and I swore to myself that nothing, no bribery or coercion, could ever wring from Will Jones the truth of Splendid Man's secret identity!

I suddenly heard Pascal speaking. "There, before you! Poxor, the world I call my own!"

Sure enough, there was a planet looming into view as the bubble began to slacken its speed. Apparently I'd been so lost in my own angry thoughts that I'd spaced out on an entire lengthy journey through the vastness of the universe. That only made me angrier.

"I imagine you know about the effects of greater gravitation and argon-free atmosphere on Earthlings," he said, and slapped a tiny device on the back of my neck. "This device will radiate you with enough antigravitons to preserve your normal strength, while injecting enough argon into your bloodstream to prevent any unwelcome changes to your scrotum."

"You think of everything," I said.

"I'm a mastermind," he said. And with that, the membrane of the space bubble dissolved and we stepped out onto the veranda of Palace Pascal, the lone edifice rising from the vine-filled jungles of Poxor.

"When I first came upon this planet, through a fortunate accident," he was saying, "I found it entirely overgrown with these creepers and populated by a savage people. But upon further exploration I discovered the ruins of a great, hyperscientific civilization. Although no historical records remain of the civilization's collapse, I can only surmise that the ignorant masses grew envious of the scientific elite and turned on them, heedless of the fact that their hubris would plunge them into ignorance and barbarism."

"More likely the elite tied itself to a short-sighted dependence on finite natural resources and ignored the need for a fair distribution of wealth and a solid foundation of social services," I said.

"Liberals," he hissed. "Anyway. What matters is that I alone had the know-how to bring the great devices of the past back to life and carve a new civilization out of the vines! I, Pox Pascal, became the savior of a world!"

Sure enough, as he stepped to the edge of the stone veranda, a great roar went up from the plaza below. There thousands of people in identical lab smocks bowed toward us chanting, "Pox!

Pox! Pox! Pox! Pox!"

"I'll bet this is one of those times you wish your parents had given you a different name," I said.

"Any name is sweet when it is chanted in obeisance," he said, with a sinister grin. "Imagine that this is a book signing at the American Booksellers' Association convention. Those peasants are the literature enthusiasts of Earth. And they're chanting, 'Will! Will! Will!'"

I could see how this guy cut it as an evil mastermind. Sure, I knew I was being manipulated all the way. But I still felt my knees get weak at the thought.

"I have influence with the New York publishing world, Will," he said. "Do you not think there are criminal masterminds in the book business? How else do you explain the success of Sidney Sheldon? I can make things happen for you, Will."

I pondered it. A multi-book deal. Maybe a National Book Award. An end to my temporary job detailing hub caps at a car wash. But I knew it couldn't be. "No thanks," I said. "I can become a literary success all by myself."

He laughed derisively.

"Okay. Then I'll become a failure by myself."

He smiled, and I knew he could see through me. "Allow me to give you the tour of Palace Pascal, Will Jones."

He led me past the giant, blast-proof doors into his windowless sanctum sanctorum. On one wall were photographs of his heroic deeds as savior of Poxor, and on the opposite wall framed newspapers recording his dastardly deeds on Earth. Scattered everywhere were the fruits of his life of pillage: piles of jewels and stacks of cash, strange artifacts from many worlds, paintings by masters from Vermeer to Picasso. Towering over all of it stood a line of giant statues of what I took to be his personal role models, the great plunderers of history. Attila the Hun. Hernán Cortés. Blackbeard. Henry Kissinger.

At a subtle move of his fingers, a mushroom-shaped flying chair cruised toward me. "Please, have a seat," he said. "We have much to discuss."

"Forget it," I said, refusing to budge. "Nothing will make me turn against my pal."

He made a noise with his tongue that might best be rendered as, "Tsk tsk," then added, "Don't you see that you and I are of a kind, Will Jones? We are men of intellect, men of culture. Why should you give your loyalty to a man of simple physical might?"

I sneered. Pretty well, too, for a guy who doesn't get a lot of practice sneering. "You're trying to tell me that's why you hate Splendid Man?"

"I oppose him because I believe in the natural elite of the intellectual. Because I see through his phony democratism and moral absolutism."

"Really," I said. "Then it has nothing to do with...your eyebrows?"

His eyes turned to stone. "Then he admits that it was he who cost me my eyebrows?"

"He says that's been your tragic obsession, Pascal. That while you were teenagers together in Turnipville, he used the heat setting of his Splendid Vision to burn away the spores of an alien mildew invasion and inadvertently singed your..."

"Inadvertently!" Pascal raised a fist and roared in rage. "As if he couldn't control his vision to the micron! Once I thought Splendid Boy and I might be allies, able to revel together in our superiority to the herd! But when he burned away my eyebrows and left me a laughing stock at Turnipville High, I knew the truth! He was nothing but another high school jock tormenting the outcast brain! And it is high time you saw the truth too!"

"Sorry," I said. "Nothing you can do will ever induce me to reveal Splendid Man's secret identity!"

He rolled his eyes. Which, from a guy without eyebrows, is a disconcerting sight. "That again! Why does he persist in thinking I want to discover his secret identity?"

"Well, you know," I said. "To strike at him through his loved ones."

He scoffed. "Through his loved ones! As if it isn't already common knowledge that he's inexplicably fixated on the reporters of the Municipalitus Daily Bolide! That he regularly rescues Pepper Pine, liberates Bobby Anderssen from bizarre transformations, and passes news scoops to that mild-mannered reporter Ken Clayton, even though, for reasons I haven't yet been able to deduce, he and Clayton are almost never seen together. All I have to do is pick up a comic book to get a full list of his loved ones!"

I have to admit, that's something I'd never thought of.

"I honestly don't care," he continued, "whether Splendid Man is secretly a scout master, a tile installer, or a Hindu mystic."

"Then what do you want from me?" I asked.

"The secret of the one faculty you have that neither I nor Splendid Man possesses. The one power that makes you so valuable to my archenemy."

I searched my memory but I wasn't coming up with anything. Surely he didn't mean the ability to craft perfect declarative sentences that had earned me a place of honor among the Array of Splendid Striplings.

"Come with me," he said, and pivoted toward the wall behind him. It slid open, revealing a vast chamber glittering with scientific equipment. I was entering the legendary laboratory of Pox Pascal! Everywhere around me rose tall beakers of bubbling fluid, spinning gyroscopes, crackling arcs of electricity, and, in the middle of it all, a towering structure covered by a metallic tarp.

"When I journeyed to ancient Alexandria to protect the world's intelligentsia from the virus of plebeian taste," he was saying, "the last person I expected to stop me was Splendid Man. I'd never have dreamed that he'd even heard of the Library of Alexandria! But when he showed up with you I discovered that my Splendid Nemesis was developing a cultural education. The thought of that musclebound buffoon imagining that he might rival me in knowledge made me want to wretch. And so I journeyed further back in time to the moment you arrived and lurked among the book stacks to eavesdrop on his plans. That's when I first heard of the secret, internal device that you use to penetrate the mysteries of literary creation. I knew the day would come when he found a way to replicate that device—and my sworn enemy would possess yet another power that Pox Pascal does not!"

"Secret, internal device?" I asked.

"I told you not to waste your *faux naïveté* on me! He asked you how you distinguish between great literature and entertaining junk, and you, foolishly imagining that no one was listening, answered him loud and clear!"

"Wait a minute," I said. "You don't mean my 'built-in shit detector'?"

The shrieking laughter he set up echoed off the walls of the laboratory. "Did you imagine that Pox Pascal would allow Splendid Man to possess a mental instrument that he himself did not? Bah! From the moment I returned to the present, I began tracking down every reference ever made to this elusive device in every library and secret laboratory to which my criminal connections gave me access! At long last, I found the first recorded mention of it!" From inside his lab coat he whipped out a yellowing magazine with a pen-and-ink drawing on the cover. "Here, in the Spring 1958 issue of an esoteric chronicle called the *Paris Review*, a global adventurer named Ernest Hemingway revealed to his ally George Plimpton that every good writer has, and I quote, 'a built-in, shock-proof shit detector.'"

"You know, you probably could have found that in a few seconds in any good reference book on writing," I said.

"Reference books!" he scoffed. "Crutches for intellectual cripples! Pox Pascal has his own ways to extract information!" Then he flung the magazine against the wall. "But curse the fool! He reveals the existence of this shit detection device but nothing about how to assemble one! I returned immediately to my laboratory on Poxor, certain that somewhere in the ancient, arcane scientific learning of this planet's vanished civilization there must have been research on the process of literary shit detection. But there was nothing! Oh, yes, I was able to develop foolproof devices for achieving perfect color harmony in a spring wardrobe and infallible musical selections for a wedding or anniversary party. And yet, for all my brilliance, literary shit detection remained beyond the reach of my highest technology!"

I shrugged. "I guess you either have it or you don't," I said.

Suddenly he whipped a weird weapon out of his lab coat and leveled it at me. I had no idea what its globular tip might do to me, but I wasn't eager to find out. "Bosh!" he roared. "And piffle! Nothing can stymie Pox Pascal when he turns his full brilliance with laser-like intensity upon a challenge! Look you now upon my greatest achievement!"

He turned the weapon on the tarp-covered structure in the middle of the lab and squeezed the trigger. There was a flash of light, and the tarp was gone, utterly disintegrated. A colossal device stood revealed, a labyrinth of coils and globes surmounted by missile-shaped towers that loomed over us like grain silos over the Kansas prairies, only different. And a lot scarier.

"Witness Pascal's Shit Detector!" he crowed. "It can process any work of literature, art, or music in a millisecond and label any portion of it as genius or feces! And thanks to these reinforced titanium plates and teflon seismic pads, it is as shock-proof as any shit detector in the known universe!" He paused to look at it and added, "Of course, I'll have to do a little miniaturization to make the built-in part work. But there will be time for that later! After I have humiliated the Man of Splendid Ignorance!"

"Whatever," I said. "But what I'm still trying to figure out is, what do you need me for?"

"Don't you know?" he cackled.

I thought for a minute. "No," I said.

"To prove its power!" he roared. "To show you that whatever shit you can detect, my machine can detect more quickly and accurately!" He tossed a paperback book at me. The cover had been ripped off, as if it had been returned for a refund by a supermarket, so I couldn't see what it was. "Read a few pages of that until you know whether it is shit or not!"

I did so. Out of the corner of my eye, I saw him fling an identical book into a sort of laundry-chute door on the side of his humongous machine. "Man," I said after a minute. "This is some smelly crap."

"Ha!" he barked. "We'll see what you know!" And with a glint of wild triumph in his eyes he pushed a button on the machine. Lights flashed, bells dinged, coils turned, and finally a little card popped out of a slot. Pascal grabbed it triumphantly and read, "Scenes of haunting eroticism strung into exquisitely told tales that deliver the cathartic pleasure of art!"

"No, it's not," I said. "It's just someone using pornography to put out a load of self-indulgent ambiguity. It doesn't work as smut or as literature. You must have pumped that machine full of academic clichés."

"Ha!" Pascal barked again. But this time I could see a faint line of sweat on his upper lip. "That happens to be a book by Anaïs Nin!"

"No wonder," I said.

He waited for me to elaborate, but I didn't see the point. His tongue darted nervously over his lips before he said, "But she's critically acclaimed as a master of eroticism and a prose stylist without peer."

I shrugged. "Critics always fall for that pseudo-artistic sexual shit."

"Oh, so you think you can trick me!" he said with a forced laugh. "You think you can make me believe that my shit detector is still inferior to yours!"

"Okay," I said. "If it makes you feel better to think so."

Now I saw his eyes narrow in what was becoming a familiar criminal-mastermind glint. "Fine, then," he said craftily. "Just for the sake of argument, let's pretend that you have in fact revealed a flaw in my masterpiece. Let's just say that you know better. What should I do to make my shit detector as accurate as yours?"

"I don't know," I said.

"Come now, my good friend," he said. "You wouldn't deny a fellow intellectual precious cultural knowledge?"

"I really don't think it's anything you can program into a machine," I said.

"All right," he said, still with that glint. "Have it your way. I'll have to fix it myself. But let's not let that spoil our visit, shall we?

Step into my parlor and share a refreshment."

Again the wall behind him opened, this time leading into a cozier, darker chamber. I saw that one wall was made entirely of glass, or, more likely, some other transparent substance much more ultrascientific than glass. Beyond it were dense jungle habitats and a startling variety of captive creatures.

"I always find it restful to look at my Poxorian menagerie when I converse," he said. "Evolution has taken such dazzling turns on this world. They fill me with hope for the future." A flying disk hissed up, carrying drinks. Pascal took one, and then the disk glided toward me. Actually, it glided a bit past me, as if leading me to my right. "So tell me, Will…if I may call you Will…when did you first notice your ability to detect shit?"

I took a step toward the disk. Then I caught myself. I realized that it floated directly opposite one particular pen in the menagerie, and that's when I tumbled to his plan. What the evil mastermind did not know was that Splendid Man, with his fondness for animals, had once described to me the fauna of Poxor that he'd come to know on one of his adventures as a fugitive on the planet pursued by misguided Poxorian citizens who believed that any foe of their beloved Pox must be an interstellar criminal. In other words, I knew a lot more about the creatures in Pascal's menagerie than he would ever have suspected.

That spiny red crustacean with the dagger-like horns thrusting from its fifteen legs, for example, was the Acrimony Beast, which had the power to spread disagreement and peevishness to all sentient beings within a five-hundred kilometer radius. That tripodal monster with the gaping hole in the center of its skull was the Forgetfulness Creature, whose amnesia gas could make a Poxorian forget his own mother.

And that one, the soft, fuzzy critter with the large, serene eyes and the mouth permanently fixed in the shape of an open smile, was the Sincerity Thing. Anyone caught in the rays that beamed from those ingenuous orbs was powerless to speak anything but the absolute truth. It was the Sincerity Thing's pen that I would have been standing directly in front of had I taken the drink offered me. Obviously Pox Pascal was hoping to weasel the truth from me by maneuvering me right smack into the path of those optical rays.

"Well," I said casually, "I suppose it was when I read *The Pearl* in eighth grade."

"Ah, *The Pearl*," he said. "A moving parable of avarice set among the modern poor."

"Actually, it's the shittiest thing Steinbeck ever wrote," I said. As I spoke, I began to pace the room as if agitated. I noticed the Sincerity Thing following me with its great, winning eyes, and I saw my chance to turn the tables on Pascal. "Anytime you have Mexicans speaking without contractions, you're in trouble. Unless you're trying to be funny."

"Then what about *The Old Man and the Sea*?"

"He was a Cuban," I said. Out of my peripheral vision I saw a golden glow building in the huge, trustworthy eyes of the Sincerity Thing, and I knew I had only seconds. I looped back in my pacing, toward a point just beyond Pascal.

"And I suppose you've been sharing the benefits of your shit detection with your Splendid Friend?" he asked snidely.

"Absolutely. He's got the makings of a pretty good shit detector in that Splendid Gut of his." And at the very moment I stepped behind Pascal, the vast, reassuring eyes of the Sincerity Thing began to pour forth their rays. A golden glow bathed the back of the villain's head. The snideness began to melt from his lips and the calculating glint faded from his eyes. Would the power of the creature really work?

"That's what hurts me most," he said softly. "The knowledge that Splendid Man can enjoy companionship and support in his literary discoveries, as rudimentary as his knowledge is, while I am locked in the loneliness of my own competitiveness and insecurity. Even as boys, what I envied most in him was his self-acceptance and ability to win affection from others, no matter what he did. Oh, yes, I envied him his ability to fly and lift volcanoes and earn himself medals as the savior of mankind again and again. But my pain ran so much deeper than that. True, I tumbled into self-loathing whenever he diverted a giant asteroid from striking Earth or subdued the radiation-deranged youth known as Strontiumite Sam or decorated the Turnipville High gym with crêpe paper for the homecoming dance in the blink of an eye. But not only then. No, I hated myself most when he would just stand there with that fluid grace in his limbs and that unguarded smile on his face, making eye contact and disarming small talk with everyone who approached him. They'd come to him trembling in awe and leave him feeling better about themselves. While I, unable to set them at ease or win their affection—because I didn't believe in my heart that I was worthy of their affection—had to settle for the brief thrill of inspiring fear and awe, a thrill that would turn to ashes in my mouth before I'd finished laughing maniacally. Did I say I envied him? It was more than envy. God, I adored him. I wanted nothing more than to hear him call me 'pal.' But in my profound feelings of inferiority I could not tolerate being but one of many whom he liked. I hungered to be the only one, I hungered to own his love! And when I could not have that, my love turned to hate, my envy to derision. Oh, God, how I adored and loathed his ease, his humility, his compassion, his good humor, and his solid common sense. How, more than anything, I worshiped and envied and despised his wholeness. That damnable way he had of seeming as though his sheer Splendidness was no great shakes and that he did not for a moment consider himself better or worse than any other student, whether it be a football star or a pom-pom girl or the president of the Logarithm Club. While my entire, fragile ego was erected on the shaky structure of my intellect! While I convinced myself that I must assert my superiority over others through sheer mental gymnastics, because that was the only way I knew to mute the voices that told me in the dead of night that I was hopelessly inadequate and utterly unlovable, that no matter how much power and notoriety I acquired with my scientific genius I would end my days alone with my anxiety, bitterness, and unspoken grief. And so I live this sham of a life, casting myself as the archenemy of the one man whose trust and respect I ever truly craved."

Yep. It worked, all right.

"So I guess this was never really about your eyebrows," I said.

He cast his eyes down in shame. "I seized upon that only to justify my resentment. The truth is, my eyebrows grew back in a couple of weeks, and I started plucking them to maintain my maimed appearance. It would have sounded fairly stupid to swear lifelong vengeance on Splendid Man because he'd caused my eyebrows to fall out for two weeks in my junior year."

"It sounds fairly stupid to swear lifelong vengeance because he caused your eyebrows to fall out under any circumstances," I said.

Around this time I began to realize that fate had handed me a once-in-a-lifetime opportunity to persuade the greatest villain in the universe to give up his life of empty power-seeking and come back to Earth as a transformed man. It would have been quite a coup, no doubt about it. Unfortunately, no sooner had I thought of it than I absent-mindedly glanced at the Sincerity Thing, and Pascal turned to see what I was looking at.

"Curses!" he roared. "You've trapped me in the ray of my own Sincerity Thing, so that I'm compelled to pour out all my hidden insecurities and self-loathings! Now I've got to break the connection and persuade you that what you were hearing was not the truth but a set of ingenious deceptions to mislead you!" Then he snorted. "Damn! I'm still doing it!"

With that he lunged for a button on the wall and brought down a colossal lead door between him and the gaze of the Sincerity Thing. He turned slowly back to me, his eyes narrowed in calculation and a sly smile on his lips. "So," he said, "I suppose you think that what you were hearing was the truth, when in fact it was merely a set of..."

"Oh, can it, Pox," I said. "We both know what's true."

Such intense hatred shot from his eyes that it seemed to light up the skin where his eyebrows should have been. "So. I suppose you're laughing at me now. I suppose you think you're better than me."

"Actually, no. I feel kind of sorry for you, but I understand."

"You...feel sorry for me?" he hissed. He whipped another weapon from his lab coat, kind of a tuning fork with a tiny radar screen on top of it, leveled it, and uttered his infamous catch phrase: "A pox on you!"

Then he pulled the trigger and everything turned white.

When I came to, I was slumped against the wall on the same street corner where I'd nearly bumped into Pox Pascal hours before. For a bleary moment, I was conscious of my disappointment that heaven looked just like the corner of 42nd and Geary, but then I realized that I hadn't actually died. And lest I should think the whole thing was a dream, there was a large, hand-scrawled note pinned to my shirt: "Someday, Will Jones, you will see that Pox Pascal can detect twice the shit you ever could! Ha ha! Signed, Pox Pascal."

I thought, "Good luck, you self-deluded fool," and went home to write.

Episode Seven
Earth's Grandest

I counted the rings anxiously, and when the connection was finally made I blurted out, "Hello! Cal! It's..." But then I realized that I had only reached his answering machine.

"Hello," his strong, steady voice intoned, "you've reached Splendid Man's Citadel of Contemplation, but I'm either matching wits with a brilliant criminal, turning back the vanguard of an invading alien armada, diverting the course of raging flood waters, or helping an ordinary citizen in need. Please leave a brief message at the sound of the beep and I'll get back to you just as soon as I can. *Beeeeep.*"

"Cal, it's me!" I said. "You've got to call me back as soon as poss..."

There was a sudden whoosh and Splendid Man was standing at my shoulder.

"But I thought you weren't there!" I said.

"I always keep my Splendid Hearing cocked to my answering machine, Will, no matter where I am. And from the urgency in your voice I decided I'd better hurry over. But tell me, why didn't you use your SOS Comb?"

"I must have left it in my shirt pocket when I took my clothes to the Rinse-O-Rama. It's probably only halfway through the dry cycle by now."

"So what seems to be the problem?"

"I just realized I'm out of milk. And money. Could you please fetch me a quart from your apartment in Municipalitus? I'll replace it as soon as I get paid tomorrow."

Without a word he zoomed out the window. And zoomed back in almost no time at all, a quart of milk in his hand. "It turned out I was all out in my Municipalitus apartment, too," he said, "but luckily I had a couple of quarts in my lunar Citadel of Contemplation."

"Gosh, Cal. I didn't mean to put you out."

"No bother at all, pal," he said. "Say, have you got anything planned for the rest of the evening?"

"Who, me?"

He removed his cape and held it toward me. "Come on," he said. "Somebody wants to meet you."

"Who?" I asked eagerly. "Please say it's Va Va Voom, your voluptuous teammate in the North American Alliance for Meetness!"

"Let's keep it a surprise," he said.

It was a short flight this time, just from one coast to the other. When he downshifted from ultrasonic speed and it was safe for me to unwrap my head, I took a peek at the earth below. I saw the lights of an enormous city that could have been Municipalitus or New York. But soon the lights fell away and we were gliding over the outskirts, passing over a series of palatial mansions with enormous grounds.

"Oh," I said dully. "Queens City. And that must be stately Brewster Manor we're zeroing in on."

"Gosh, Will. I thought you'd be excited about meeting Catman."

"I will be," I said. "Just as soon as I get over my disappointment that he's not Va Va Voom."

"Duck your head."

I did, and we whooshed through a window. A moment later we alit in a vast, oak-paneled drawing room where a man reposed before a blazing log fire, a sleeping hound curled at his feet. He stood at our approach, and I saw that he was precisely Splendid Man's height. Above the waist he wore a satin smoking jacket and an ascot. Below, I saw the tights of his Catman costume and boots of tabby-fur.

"Wyatt Brewster," Splendid Man said, "I'd like you to meet my pal, Will Jones."

"Honored," I said.

Wyatt had a firm handshake, but it wasn't one of those bone-crusher grips. His face was rather square, his features even and strong, his ears curiously small and set close to the sides of his head.

He was staring into my eyes intently. I'd never encountered such a penetrating gaze. I felt as if he could see into my inmost self, down to the very molecules of my DNA. And then I realized what he must have been up to. Being the world's greatest detective, he was storing everything his keen eye could glean of my character into his mental crime files so that, should I ever turn to a life outside the law, he would know how best to go about bringing me to justice.

"You have striking eyes," he said.

"Oh," I said. "Gee, thanks."

"Remind me to teach you some eye exercises I developed that will restore your vision to 20-20, if you practice them diligently. It's a shame to hide such a glittering cerulean behind a pair of discount Cardins. You don't want to look like Ken Clayton, do you?"

"Did I warn you that Wyatt can be disconcertingly direct?" Cal put in.

I turned and saw that Splendid Man had already sat down in one of two armchairs that flanked Wyatt's own. He picked up one of a pair of snifters from a small table and took a sip of amber liquid. That's when it hit me that I'd interrupted their evening together. "Oh, no," I said to Cal. "I'm butting in on you and Mr. Brewster, aren't I?"

"Mr. Brewster was my murdered father's name," Wyatt said. "Please call me Wyatt. And would you mind if I call you William? I'm inordinately fond of the name William."

"I don't mind," I said. "I'm awfully sorry to have called Cal away."

"I'm glad you did," said Wyatt. "I've been wanting to meet you for ages, and it was I who suggested that Calv'In bring you here when your summons came through. The emergency wasn't too dire, I hope?"

"Er...not too," I said.

"Cognac?"

"Please."

He yanked on a pull chord, and an elderly man who looked remarkably like Alec Guinness stepped in and stood expectantly at attention. So closely did he resemble the great actor, in fact, that I wondered if he was one of the dead ringers for Earth people from Strontor, the City in the Can, whom Splendid Man had somehow restored to full size.

"A splash of the *Très Vieille* for William, Alec."

"Immediately, Master Wyatt," he said, and padded off soundlessly.

When Wyatt and I had sat down he said, "Calv'In tells me that you're a cheese grater at Domino's."

"Well, temporarily, of course."

"Of course. I understand you want to be a writer."

"Well," I said, fidgeting, "I do like to..."

"Tell me, have you ever written any short-short stories? I'm awfully keen on the form."

"Uh, no. I can't say that I..."

"And I adore absurdist fiction. You've read Donald Barthelme, to be sure?"

"Absolutely," I said. "I like him very..."

"And have you ever tried to emulate his...approach to fiction, shall we say?"

"Well, now that you mention it, there was one story called..."

"Of course you agree that the master of the short form was Henry James. Not only for his ingenuity of construction but for his skill at weaving a taboo subtext between the lines of his narratives where only the most astute eye can discern it."

"Well, I have to admit that James's style has always left me cold," I said, with a smile I hoped wasn't too smug, "but I do pride myself on my ability to spot a subtext that most people would miss."

He gazed at me a moment and then smiled. "I have no doubt

that you do," he said. "I'll be interested to hear what subtexts you can pick out of tonight's conversation."

"Now, Wyatt," Cal said, with something that almost sounded like a warning.

Wyatt leaned forward, his gimlet eyes boring into me again. "And to what do you attribute this acuity, William, a unique power or rigorous training?"

The return of Alec with my cognac saved me from Wyatt's third degree. For a minute there I'd had a taste of what the Cat-Eared Combatant's enemies, like the Punster or Bipolar, must have endured under his remorseless interrogation. I thanked the stars that no strange quirk of fate had indeed turned me to a life of crime.

My respite was brief, however, as Wyatt started in again. "And what do you think of the absurdist style known as 'camp,' William? You know, before my friend Susan Sontag popularized the term, it had a genuine…"

"Oh, zip it," said Splendid Man. "I've already told Will how much you know about everything. You can stop trying to impress him."

Wyatt sighed and sat back in his chair. "Ah, the man knows my foibles all too well."

"I'll say I do," Splendid Man said. "Now settle down for a spell."

But Wyatt was coming erect in his chair again. "I've got a bone to pick with William first," he said, and turned to me. "Calv'In used to be such a good listener when I was in the mood to pontificate on art and literature. But since you've taken him under your wing, he now has the temerity to interrupt me with opinions of his own. Why, just last week, he wanted to argue the finer points of Nietzsche's notion of the superman."

A warm glow filled me. After all Splendid Man had done for me, it was certainly gratifying to hear that I'd given him something of value in return.

"Just don't pat yourself on the back too strenuously, dear boy," Wyatt continued. "I guarantee that if you ever stop recommending books to him, he'll be back reading whatever he sees at the supermarket checkout counter within a week."

I looked across Wyatt's body at Cal to see how he was taking these gibes, but to my surprise he was just gazing at the fire and chuckling softly. I realized that I had never seen him looking so much at ease. Slumped down on the base of his spine as he was, his legs stretched straight out with his red boots crossed at the ankles, his hand lazily swirling the cognac in his snifter, he presented a picture of a man entirely at peace with the world. Everyone knows that Splendid Man and Catman often fight crime together as Earth's Grandest Duo, but I'd always assumed that their partnership was confined to the business of defending justice. After all, Wyatt Brewster doesn't have any Ps in his name. Only now did I understand what close friends they must truly be. I couldn't help feeling a little jealous, even as I felt honored to share with them an evening at home of the sort they must have enjoyed a thousand times before.

For a while we sat in silence, listening to the crackling of the flames and basking in the serenity. Of course it was Wyatt who shattered the spell. "You just passed a significant test of mine, William. You've demonstrated the rare talent—one, I must add, of which I myself am bereft—of sitting quietly in a hushed room. To quote Pascal…"

"Man's unhappiness," I said, glad to be interrupting him for a change, "stems from his inability to sit quietly in his room."

Wyatt arched an eyebrow in my direction. "Bravo, William."

"Pascal said that?" asked Cal. "Pox Pascal, the evil scientific genius who's been my archenemy since boyhood?"

Wyatt looked incredulous for a moment, then burst into gales of laughter.

"Oh, calm down, silly man," Cal said. "I know you're talking about that Frenchman, Blaise Pascal. Will lent me a copy of his *Pensées* last summer. I was just playing the bumpkin because I know you enjoy it so much."

When Wyatt had regained his breath he said, "After all these years, you can still surprise me. Never let it be said that the Dusklit

Deducer can never be fooled—or worse, wouldn't enjoy it!"

They clinked glasses and drank.

We heard a door open, then high-pitched titters, and a moment later a young man in slacks and a v-neck sweater escorted a very pretty teenage girl into the room.

"Hi, Wyatt. Hi, Splendid Man," he said. "I'd like you to meet Muffy."

"Y-Y-You know Splendid Man?" Muffy sputtered.

"An old friend of the family," the young man said matter-of-factly, but not without a trace of cockiness.

We were all on our feet.

"Delighted to meet you, my dear," Wyatt said. "Muffy, Greg, this is William Jones."

And I realized that the young man was none other than Greg Dickson, Wyatt Brewster's young ward and, when in his secret identity of Sparrow, the Pugnacious Prodigy, his partner in crime fighting.

"Oh, yeah, the writer," Greg said.

"Well…" I started to say, but Wyatt broke in, adding, "He does like to write, to be sure. Now, can I have Alec bring you young folks anything? Bosco, Sno Balls, whatever it is you children indulge in these days?"

"*Bosco?*" Greg retorted. "Holy shit, Wyatt!"

"Away with you and your sailor's tongue," said Wyatt with a flick of his wrist. "Those who are old enough to have developed some manners are attempting to hold a conversation."

With a barking laugh and some rude remark about "sailors' tongues," Greg ushered his friend out of the room. We soon heard their feet tramping up a flight of stairs.

"I worry about that lad," Wyatt said, resuming his place before the fire. "He's just turned sixteen and every night that we're not on patrol he brings home a different conquest. I only hope he has the sense to don the proper equipment before he plunges into the fray."

"Gosh, I wonder who he takes after," Cal said.

"Now, let's not get catty," Wyatt said

"Not me, Mr. Catman sir," Cal said.

"Oh, ho! Now we're getting word-play out of the big oaf!" chortled Wyatt. "I tell you, William, your influence on this man has been nothing short of pernicious."

I was enjoying the repartee—now that I was no longer the focal point—and hated to cut it short, but what I'd seen left me with no choice.

"Excuse me, fellas," I said. "But I think you should look out that window."

They craned their necks to look past the sumptuous velvet drapes bordering the window I indicated. There, above the gnarled silhouettes of trees, clearly limned against the starry backdrop, glowed the giant silhouette of a cat, one paw outstretched and slightly curled, as if poised to strike—the redoubted Cat Signal!

"How dreary," Wyatt said. "The commissioner must have known we were having too pleasant an evening."

In spite of his words, he came to his feet in an instant, peeling off his smoking jacket to reveal the lithe, pearly costume beneath. He unwound the ascot, and it flowed into an ominously billowing cape. Finally, he reached behind his neck and pulled over his head the feline cowl that has struck fear into the hearts of countless criminals. There before me stood the Secretive Sentinel himself in full regalia.

"To the Catcave, gentlemen!"

The hound had slept like a brick all evening, but suddenly it leapt to attention. I saw that it wore a mask over his eyes.

"Go back to sleep, boy," Wyatt said, patting the dog's head. "William should be able to provide us with all the assistance we'll require tonight."

As the dog curled up again, Wyatt turned and touched a hidden stud on the wall and a panel slid aside to reveal two fireman's poles. Wyatt and I each took one while Cal floated down beside us. A moment later we landed in a...garage?

"Forgive my little joke, William," Wyatt said, noting my disappointment. "There isn't such a thing as a Catcave. All my scientific equipment, crime files, mementos, and trophies fit easily into that monstrosity upstairs I call home. Yes, even the giant subway token. I've just loved saying that line ever since Manu East, who played me on the television show these long years ago, delivered it with such *élan*."

The Catmobile didn't let me down, though. It was as futuristic-looking, as sleek and finny, as the comics had always portrayed it to be.

"William and I will take the Catmobile," Wyatt said to Splendid Man. "You can fly alongside."

But Cal shook his head. "I think I'd better drive," he said. "With my invulnerable brain cells..."

"Yes, yes," Wyatt interrupted, "alcohol has no effect on your mood or behavior. But you're right. It does on mine, and I must confess to being a trifle embalmed. William, to the rumble seat!"

We all piled in, the rocket engines roared to life, and Cal guided the Catmobile down the long tunnel that led from Brewster Manor to a distant exit cleverly disguised as the mouth of an abandoned asbestos mine. Soon we were driving along a deserted country road toward the distant lights of Queens City.

"Any idea what the trouble might be?" asked Cal.

"Some so-called archvillain or other, to be sure. That's all Commissioner Kitchener ever calls me out on any longer. He can't seem to get it through his head that any rookie cop walking a beat could take down these costumed popinjays in a second."

"Have you heard of any prison breaks in the area?"

"Pox Pascal and Cerebriac break out of prison, Calv'In. The pathetic jokers I put away stay put. Of course, I don't jail all the clowns I apprehend," he added. "Some I douse with gasoline and burn alive." He cackled piercingly.

"Let's not get started on Hollywood," Cal said.

"No," Wyatt agreed. "Let's not."

Before long we were driving through the city limits. As we neared police headquarters, Wyatt said, "Let me warn you. The old commish is in his dotage, I'm afraid. Don't mind me if I start acting according to his expectations. I like to jolly the old boy along. Bring a little sunshine into the autumn of his life, you know."

When the three of us burst into the commissioner's office, Catman did a peculiar skip-jump and came to rest at attention by his desk, his arms crossed over his chest so that one hand gripped each shoulder. Commissioner Kitchener was a dried-up little prune of a man. Beside him stood an aging Irish bull in harness.

"Ah, Splendid Man!" Kitchener quavered. "How good to see Earth's Grandest heroes together again!" Then he noticed me. "But why is the Pugnacious Prodigy out of uniform?"

"His jerkin is at the cleaners," Catman said. "What seems to be the trouble?"

"We've got quite a mess on our hands, Catman!" the old man said.

"Saints alive, that we do!" added the bull.

"A new malevolent villainess calling herself Batwoman and her gang of costumed cutthroats broke into the Stroganoff Import Company warehouse on Drayage Street—just after they'd gotten in a secret shipment of rare sapphires all the way from Malaysia! Before the crooks could escape with the loot, a squad of our boys happened by and boxed them up inside! But, curse the luck, they've got hostages!"

"Saints preserve us," croaked the bull, "that they do!"

Catman drove a fist hard into the palm of his other hand. "The fiends!" he shouted, his voice rising into a weird ululation.

Splendid Man caught my eye and winked.

"We're bringing in a hostage negotiator as we speak!" said Kitchener.

"Forget the hostage negotiator," Catman said. "We'll take care of things." He turned to Splendid Man and me and intoned, "Gentleman, to the Catmobile!"

As soon as we were out in the hall Splendid Man and Catman started giggling like girls. They laughed so hard that I practically had to support them down to the car. Only then did they calm down. As Splendid Man pointed the car toward the warehouse district, Catman seemed downright laconic.

"Are you always this mellow when you go into action?" I asked.

"It's these supposed master villains that bore me," he said. "You can have all your Conundrummers and your Venus Flytraps and your Emus. 'Conundrum me this,' my ass. I wouldn't crap into a thimble for the lot of them. Give me a case of political corruption or corporate malfeasance any day. There are your real villains these days. Congressmen who trade their votes for campaign cash, captains of industry who befoul the very air and water their own children will have to breathe and drink, politicians who manipulate a hostage crisis to determine the outcome of an election, a president who breaks the back of a once proud labor union, foul plans afoot to cut taxes on the rich while slashing social programs for the poor, the rise of the so-called Moral Majority. Just don't get me started!"

"Boy," I said, "now I know why they call you the Masked Muckraker!"

He turned around and looked at me where I sat scrunched up in the rumble seat. "No one ever called me the Masked Muckraker," he said.

"I know," I said. "I just made it up."

He glanced at Splendid Man. "I like your pal."

"He is a fine pal," Cal said.

Wyatt turned back at me. "May I borrow it?"

"I'd be honored," I said.

We arrived at the Stroganoff Import warehouse and piled out of the car. My legs had fallen asleep and I almost fell on my face. A bunch of cops surrounded us.

"Are the hostages still in there?" Catman asked.

"Yes, sir," a young patrolman answered breathlessly.

Catman said, "Splendid Man," and Splendid Man vanished.

In the distance, we heard the tinkle of broken glass.

"The hostage negotiator should be here any minute," another cop put in.

"Tell him to go home," Catman said, just as Splendid Man reappeared, two hostages under each arm.

"Is that all of them?" Catman asked.

"Yes," Splendid man said. "Shall I round up the fiends?"

"Let me try something first."

Catman borrowed a bullhorn from an officer. "This is Catman talking," he said into it. "We have the hostages. In three minutes, we're going to douse the building with gasoline and burn it to the ground. Over and out."

In less than a minute they all came dashing out the door, tripping over each other in their haste. I guess they'd all seen the movie.

These "Bat Boys," as we later learned they called themselves, were just a bunch of rowdies wearing striped shirts and bat ears. They meekly allowed themselves to be herded into a waiting paddy wagon, nary a BAM or a ZAP required.

Then, last of all, came the Batwoman. When I saw her my heart nearly stopped. Sheathed from head to toe in a black leather jumpsuit that followed every undulation of her willowy frame, she moved with the long-legged grace of a Broadway dancer. As an officer guided her into the black mariah, she stopped suddenly and made sizzling eye contact with Catman.

"Don't you want to handcuff me yourself, Calico Crusader?"

The cops whistled, wiped their brows melodramatically, and pulled at their shirts as if to indicate a sudden heat wave, but Catman only yawned. What self-control, to resist an innuendo from a woman like that!

Crestfallen, the villainess slunk into the dark van. The police thanked Catman and Splendid Man profusely—and me too, to my embarrassment—and we took our leave. Despite his contempt for costumed criminals, Catman seemed well pleased with himself on the drive back.

"Did you see those buffoons come scrambling out of there?" he said.

Cal chuckled. "In a bit of a fright, weren't they?"

"A fright? They pooped their tight little pants!"

"Maybe we should feel grateful to the folks in Hollywood after all," said Cal. "They might make our jobs a lot easier if all our foes believed their portrayals of us."

"Three cheers for Jerry Jacobs!" said Wyatt.

"That jerk wrote your movie, too?" I asked.

"'Batwoman,'" Cal mused. "What will they think of next?"

"She sure was a doll, though," I said. "You guys have to admit that!" Wyatt spun around in his seat and impaled me with another of his penetrating stares. "Is this a joke, or have you honestly never realized that your friend Cal and I are…"

I saw Splendid Man shoot him a glance, and Wyatt's eyes softened. "…duty bound never to think of a villain in anything but the most professional manner?"

We all laughed, but a bit forcedly. I got the distinct impression that Wyatt had been about to say something different until he caught Cal's look, something, perhaps, that would have confirmed the rumors of the throbbing erotic undercurrents that entangled him and his most glamorous female foes. I understood then that there were secrets within the fraternity of heroes to which even I, Splendid Man's pal, was not privy.

Back at Brewster Manor, we took our seats again before the fire that Alec had kept banked in our absence. We sipped our cognac and sometimes we talked politics and sometimes we talked literature and sometimes we didn't talk at all. This went on into the wee hours, and if I live to be a hundred years old I don't believe I'll ever spend a grander and stranger night on this earth.

Episode Eight
Will's Trip to Turnipville

I took a day off from my temporary job breading shrimp at Long John Silver's to watch *Leave it to Beaver*. I noticed it in the TV listings and I couldn't resist. This one was from one of the earlier seasons, before Beaver's head and teeth got too big and made him ugly. In this episode, Eddie Haskell and Wally had seen a movie about a mad hypnotist and Eddie was attempting to talk Beaver into trying to hypnotize him. Wally was saying, "Aw, don't listen to him, Beav, he's just giving you the business," when someone tapped on my second-story window.

"Come in, Cal," I called.

The window was unlatched, and with a puff of Splendid Breath, Splendid Man blew it open and swooped in. "Hello, Will. As I was streaking over the city at Splendid Speed I heard your TV go on and thought I'd drop in. What are you watching?"

"I'm surprised you don't recognize it," I said. "It's *Leave it to Beaver*, a popular family situation comedy first aired in the late fifties."

"I'm afraid I don't have much time to watch TV," said Splendid Man. "Of course, I could process the images at Splendid Speed, just as I do with books. But I've never been able to lick the technical problem of playing the video cassettes fast enough without setting them on fire."

"Uh huh," I said.

Eddie Haskell called Beaver a squirt. Wally said, "Aw, lay off him, Eddie." Eddie replied, "Listen, Sam, can I help it if he's a squirt?"

Cal looked at me quizzically. "This seems a little unsophisticated for your taste, Will," he said.

"It isn't the humor that draws me to this program," I explained. "The world of Beaver Cleaver and his family represents a vision of childhood in small-town America for which every American secretly yearns when the terrors of modern city life become too great to bear."

"I don't understand, Will," said Cal, brow furrowed. "What vision of childhood is that?"

"You'll find a similar yearning for this impossibly idealized upbringing in the works of Tarkington, Saroyan, and Bradbury," I said. "Although I know such a life could never exist in reality, I find myself wishing I had spent my youth in a small town of bungalows and stately Victorian homes, neighbors greeting each other from their porch swings, streets dappled by the sun through the leaves of grand old elms, long summer afternoons of adventures both real and fancied, a willow-lined stream with a fine swimming hole, clean-living boisterous boys and coquettish girls in skirts, the tinkle of lemonade being stirred behind porch screens, the friendly cop on the corner and the old professor who invents things on his front porch, waking on a rosy dawn to smell the dewy grass and see the sun warming the bright flower beds of the house next door, kindly old folks who share their chocolate milk and their son's old comic books with the neighborhood kids, the smell of sausage in the morning, of tomato soup at lunch, and of fresh-baked cherry pie cooling on the window sill late on a summer evening that never seems to end."

"Why, Will!" exclaimed Cal. "That sounds exactly like my childhood!"

"You're pulling my leg," I said.

"Of course I'm not, Will. You're the jokester of our little friendship. What you describe is the very picture of Turnipville, the town where I grew up. Haven't you read about it in *Splendid Boy* comics?"

"Well, sure, but I figured the publishers were just whitewashing things to mollify parents, or something."

"Quite the contrary," he said. "They offer a perfect portrait of the town where Stronto and I were fortunate enough to splash down in our Strontiumese space ark. And even more fortunately, we did so after the public swimming pool had closed for the day, so no one was there but one kindly municipal maintenance man."

Suddenly there was a catch in his voice and the glint of unshed tears in his eyes. I respectfully kept my silence, knowing that he was thinking of that maintenance man and his warm-hearted wife, Pa and Ma Clayton, whose deaths he had unwittingly caused when he'd left them to vacation on a Pacific atoll having forgotten that it was soon to be vaporized in an A-bomb test.

Splendid Man sat down in my rocking chair that doesn't rock anymore and stared in the direction of my ceiling, a faraway look in his eyes. "I often miss my life there very much," he said. "Although I never really fit in, of course. I was so different from other boys, and even though I felt a powerful fondness for Roswell Smutts, my boyhood pal, I could never tell him how I felt. And it was a tremendous burden having to keep such a huge secret at that age. I don't know what I would have done without Ma and Pa's kindness and understanding. People don't realize how extraordinary it was, back in those days, for them to accept me so calmly for what I really was."

For a minute I didn't know what the heck he was talking about, but then it hit me. I hadn't thought about it before, but now I realized that the Claytons had taken an alien from outer space into their home and loved and cherished him as a son. And this years before movies like *E.T.* had paved the way.

"But surely your courtship of Patti Pert, that blazing redhead, must have helped chase away the blues," I said.

Splendid Man gave me an odd look. Then he sighed and said, "Well, she certainly provided a distraction, Will. You can't imagine how indefatigable she was in trying to prove Ken Clayton was really Splendid Boy, and how much time and energy I expended in devising ruses and ploys to lead her astray. And, in her own way, she was certainly endearing."

"By the way, Cal, I've always been meaning to ask you. Did you go straight from Splendid Boy to Splendid Man, or were you Splendid Teen in between?"

"Of course I was, Will. And those years, just as they are for so many people, were the hardest of my life. But can you imagine a comic book called, *Splendid Teen, the Adventures of Splendid Man When He Was an Adolescent?*"

"It does sound rather sickening, now that you mention it," I agreed. "But your boyhood, even taking into account the alienation and all, still sounds pretty ideal to me."

He gave me another odd look and said, "Yes, Will. I can see how it would sound that way to *you*."

"I know what, Cal," I said. "Why don't we take a little trip to Turnipville?"

"It's not the same, Will," he said. "Like so many other small towns across the nation, it's fallen victim to creeping suburbanization. I'm afraid you can't tell it apart from Sunnyvale or Hayward today. Sometimes I wonder if things could have been much worse if my archenemy Pox Pascal had actually succeeded in any of his mad schemes to conquer the world."

"I meant back in time, Splendid Man. Back to the days when you were a boy."

Splendid Man's brow furrowed. "Oh no, Will. That would set up too many time paradoxes. It just wouldn't do at all for my boyhood self to meet me face to face. It would leave too many emotional scars if he found out that he was going to be unwittingly responsible for Ma and Pa Clayton's demise."

"I know, Cal. We'll just pick a point in time when Splendid Boy was off on a mission in space or on one of his many visits to the 30th Century where he shared countless colorful adventures with his pals in the Array of Splendid Striplings, among whose ranks I, as Literary Lad, now number as an honorary member. So to speak."

"I still have my doubts, Will," Splendid Man said. "But if it'll make you really happy, I hate to say no to a pal."

"Thanks, pal," I said.

The short trip back through the decades passed in an instant. Splendid Man had barely wrapped me in his indestructible cape when he was already unwrapping my face. The wind of our flight whipped my hair around my eyes as we circled over Turnipville. Below us was a small town of bungalows and stately Victorian homes, the streets dappled by the sun through the leaves of grand old elms. The dog in a red cape who took flight in pursuit of an airplane was a discordant element, but still I was charmed.

Splendid Man brought us down below the church steeple, explaining, "I'll put you up with some old friends of my foster parents, a nice family with two boys. I hope you understand that I'd love to put you up with Ma and Pa Clayton, Will, but I can't risk you accidentally blurting out the details of their demise, for which I was unwittingly responsible. It might cast a cloud over their autumn years."

A mushroom cloud, I thought, but I kept it to myself. "Sure, Cal," I said sincerely. "I understand."

We made our way along a willow-lined stream and past a fine swimming hole. You didn't need Splendid Hearing to hear the tinkling of lemonade being stirred behind every screen door. Nor did you need it to hear an evil cackling coming from somewhere amidst the willows, which I immediately recognized as what Pox Pascal's voice would have sounded like when he'd been a teen, but I paid it no heed. At last we came to an especially quaint bungalow with a Buick parked in the driveway.

"To avoid a time paradox," Splendid Man explained, "you go up to the door alone while I streak up to space and, disguising my voice as Splendid Boy's, address these folks with my power of Splendid Voice Casting."

I knocked on the door and a middle-aged man dressed in slacks, golf sweater, and tie answered. Thrusting his hands into his pockets and gently rocking back and forth on the balls of his feet, he said, "Why, you must be the new sales boy for American Seeds! You know, the last boy showed so much pep and zest that he sold ninety-six packets in one afternoon and won many valuable prizes!"

"Actually, I'm…er…" I began.

The ersatz voice of Splendid Boy suddenly boomed all around us. "Excuse me folks. This is Splendid Boy, speaking from outer space. I've been contaminated by a space virus deadly to all human life. Until I can bathe myself in a decontamination spray, the ingredients for which exist only in a distant galaxy, I'll have to avoid contact with you. This is my friend Will Jones, who just took the train in from Azure Valley and needs a place to stay. I hope this won't put you folks out."

"Why, of course not!" said the man, addressing the skies. "Any friend of Splendid Boy's is a friend of the Babbitts!" He turned to me and said, "Come on in, Will, and meet Mrs. Babbitt and the boys!"

Mr. Babbitt took me across an immaculately tidy living room and into the kitchen. An attractive woman in a chiffon dress, frilly apron, high heels, and pearls stood in front of the stove stirring tomato soup in a pot.

"Will Jones," Mr. Babbitt said, "this is my lovely wife, May Babbitt."

"Good afternoon, Mrs. Babbitt," I said.

She smiled sweetly and said, "Help yourself to some milk and cookies, Will."

As I opened the refrigerator and drew out a big pitcher of ice-cold milk, Mrs. Babbitt said to her husband, "Warren, why don't you call the boys so that they can meet Will?"

Warren clapped his hands, rubbed them vigorously, and said, "Why, what a good-neighborly gesture, May!" He went to the foot of the stairs and hollered, "Boys! Boys! Come down here! I want you to meet someone!"

"Be right down, Dad," called the nasal voice of a teenager. We heard the thunder of their feet running down the stairs and then Mr. Babbitt introduced me to a high school kid in a letterman sweater and a little boy wearing a baseball cap.

"Will, these are my fine boys, Walter and the Rabbit!"

"My, what an unusual name," I said.

"His real name is Bill, but Walter couldn't pronounce it when he was little."

As Mr. Babbitt spoke, the little boy smiled, revealing a bucktoothed grin.

Walter rubbed his nose with his forefinger and said, "Hey Dad, me and Freddy Hoskins and Stumpy Stableford are gonna go over to Marshall's Field and mess around."

Mr. Babbitt frowned at Walter and said, "Why Walter, how uncivil of you! Shouldn't you invite our guest to go along?"

Walter rubbed his nose again and asked, "Gee, Will, do you like to play softball and junk too?"

"Sure," I said. "I used to be a pitcher in Little League."

The Rabbit piped in, "I used to play in Little League too, until I poked Harry Mortadello in the stomach and Miss Cinders yelled at me and made me go see the principal, Mrs. Rugburn."

"Well, leave it to Rabbit!" Mr. Babbitt put in jovially.

"Hey Walter, can I hang around with you guys?" whined Rabbit, fiddling with his baseball cap.

"But Rabbit," said Mrs. Babbitt. "I thought you wanted to go over to the Claytons' house to drink chocolate milk and read their son Ken's old comic books."

"Aw gee, Mom," said Rabbit. "I can do that anytime. A neat guy like Will doesn't come around every day!"

"Why thank you, Rabbit," I said.

As I left the house flanked by the two brothers, May called from the kitchen, "Now don't be late for dinner, boys!"

"No, ma'am!" I called.

As we walked along, Rabbit gaped at my beard with eyes like saucers. "Gee, Will," he chirped, "I've never known a guy with real whiskers before! How did you do it?"

I winked at Walter and said, "Just you wait, Rabbit. In a few years, you'll be able to grow whiskers of your own."

"*Really*, Will?" he squealed. "No foolin'?"

"Well, sure, goof!" laughed Walter. "If mom and dad ever let you!"

Rabbit charged at Walter, and they chased each other around the bushes all the way to the park. As I greeted the friendly cop on the corner and waved to the old professor tinkering with a time machine on his front porch, I wondered whether the innate decency of Turnipville had helped young Calv'In grow into the Splendid

Man he is, or whether it was Splendid Boy's presence that somehow kept the town so ideal. Whatever the case, with every step I grew more certain that this was the place for me.

We found the park full of clean-living boisterous boys and coquettish girls in skirts, the boys engaged in a furious but friendly game of ball and the girls glowing in admiration. Lurking by the monkey bars I caught sight of an evil-looking boy with glowing silvery skin whom I realized must be the tormented and irradiated Strontiumite Sam, but I tuned him out.

"There's Freddy Hoskins!" Walter called, indicating a curly-haired teen with a superior smirk pasted on his face, and we all ran over to greet him.

And then I saw her.

Even though she was dressed in a boy's shirt, a woolen skirt, bobby sox, and saddle shoes, even though she was only sixteen years old and her pixyish face had never known make-up, the resemblance to Rita Hayworth took my breath away.

"You must be Patti Pert, Splendid Boy's girl," I said to the incendiary redhead before me.

"You bet she is!" said the curly-haired youth behind me. "And now that I've decided to reveal my secret identity, she'll be Freddy Hoskins's girl!"

"Oh, Freddy, don't be such a goof," Patti said. "You can't really expect me to believe a creep like you could be Splendid Boy."

"Aw, he's just giving you the business," Walter said.

"Creep creep creep!" Rabbit chirped.

"Oh, yeah?" Freddy said. "Watch this, Gertrude!"

Freddy suddenly turned and scampered up a grand old elm. Running out on a high branch, I saw him discreetly tie balloons to his limbs and hurl himself into space. It might have worked, if just then a flock of birds, mistaking the balloons for their natural enemies, hadn't popped them with their beaks. Amid gasps of horror, Freddy plummeted earthward, cleaving the air with his "Yiiiiiiiiiiiiiiiiiiiii!"

I was the closest to him, and instinctively I ran to catch him—

but I was too far away to do any good. Then, just before he hit the ground, a gust of wind formed a cushion beneath his feet and lowered him softly. I realized it must have been Splendid Man's doing, as he kept up a vigil from outer space with his Splendid Vision.

The rest of the gang caught up to us. "Gee Will!" Walter exclaimed. "How did you do that?"

"Well, it happened so fast, I…er…don't know."

Patti looked at me shrewdly.

Freddy, cringing in humiliation, lowered his curly head and slunk off amid catcalls of "Creep creep creep!"

"Holy cow, Will," said Patti. "You sure are brave."

"Oh…I wouldn't say that," I mumbled.

"Would you like someone to show you the sights in Turnipville, Will?"

"Why, sure."

"Then come pick me up after dinner. I'll let you take me out for a soda." She winked, spun on her heel, and sashayed away. I couldn't help noticing that the other guys looked at me with something like awe.

Soon the game broke up, and I followed the boys back to the Babbitt house, once again watching them chase each other around and around the bushes. Over a delicious dinner of tomato soup, pot roast, and canned peas, the boys related the day's adventures while Mr. Babbitt spoke proudly of his golf score. I cleaned my plate of every crumb as May Babbitt looked on in delight.

I took advantage of a break in the conversation to excuse myself and announce that I had a date with Patti Pert. As I let myself out the front door, I overheard Mr. Babbitt say, "Gosh all fishhooks! Leave it to Will!"

I smelled cherry pies cooling on every windowsill as I walked the quiet lane. Suddenly, Splendid Man swooped down before me.

"Will," he said, "I took a little peek into the future and saw that Splendid Boy and the Array of Splendid Striplings, that august company to which you belong in an honorary capacity, have just defeated Dr. Grasshopper Gorgo and his Fantastic Chemoids. I can't risk being here when he returns. We should be going."

"But, Cal," I whined. "I'm on my way to a date with Patti Pert!"

"You're putting me on, Will. A man your age going out with a sixteen-year-old girl?"

"But it's not *her* I'm interested in," I whimpered. "It's this town and this era. The long afternoons of adventures both real and fancied, waking on a rosy dawn to smell the dewy grass and see the sun warming the bright flowers of the house next door..."

"But you can't stay," said Cal. "What would people think if you disappeared from San Francisco as a twenty-six year old, only to turn up as a middle-aged man in Turnipville?" "I'm sorry to create such a time paradox," I said. "But I'm not going to give up the good life now that I've found it! Besides, Scribner's was still a genuinely literary publisher in this era, not a producer of run-of-the-mill junk. This could be the beginning of my career as a novelist, Cal! If Scribner's published Thomas Wolfe, they'll publish me. Wolfe's dialogue was wooden, too."

"Well, if you're going to be stubborn," Splendid Man said, "maybe I'd better create a cosmic disturbance to delay Splendid Boy's return to Turnipville for a few hours."

Splendid Man flew away and I continued on my stroll. At the stately Victorian home of the Pert family, I found Patti in her prettiest dress. A ribbon nestled in her hair. Professor Pert, the world-renowned entomologist, saw us to the door and bid us a good time.

As we strolled along, she introduced me to the Andersons, the Stones, the Douglases, and the Smuttses, all on their porch swings. We came to a little place called Krazy Karl's Malt Shoppe and took two seats at the counter. The kindly soda jerk gave us a little extra whipped cream and two straws. As we lowered our heads toward the glass, Patti suddenly grabbed me by the hair and pulled down, jabbing the straw into my eye.

"Yeeeeow!" I said.

Patti, paying no attention to my scream, calmly asked the soda jerk to bring her a fork. She took it from him and without a moment's hesitation stabbed it into my hand.

"Aiiiiieee!" I said.

She reached into her little purse and brought out a book of matches. Nonchalantly, she struck one and held it to my beard, which promptly burst into flames.

"Yipes!" I said, sticking my chin into the soda to douse the fire.

"That proves it!" Patti said. "The fact that your beard burns proves that it's false!"

"What in the world are you talking about?"

"Do you think I'm stupid?" she snapped. "I've noticed that you're never around when Splendid Boy is in action!"

"But I've never been here at all until today!"

"Don't try to confuse me," she said. "I saw you save Freddy Hoskins with your Splendid Breath today."

"That wasn't me, it was…" I started to say, but I never got to finish the sentence. Patti was pulling a .32 caliber Walther PPK pistol out of her purse. "Omigosh!" I cried. Bullets whizzed past my head as I dashed for the door.

I reached the street, vibrated the teeth of my SOS Comb, and Splendid Man swooped down, bundling me up in his arms.

"Holy cow!" I said, as we took to the skies. "Patti tried to shoot me!"

"Yes," Splendid Man said. "When that girl gets an idea in her head she can be quite a pest. Maybe now you'll be willing to go home."

I glanced at the twinkling lights of the town below us and sighed in mourning for the life I could never have.

"Shouldn't we say goodbye to the Babbitts?" I asked.

"We'd better not," Splendid Man said. "Splendid Boy should have defeated the Arcturian Hellhounds I secretly unleashed on him by now and he'll be returning any minute. I'll just burn a note into the Babbitts' front door with my Splendid Vision explaining that you had to leave because Scribner's called you to New York to discuss your book. A little white lie never hurt anybody."

After he burned the message, Splendid Man accelerated for our trip home. Unwrapping his cape from my eyes, I caught a glimpse of the Babbitt boys through their bedroom window. Walter and the Rabbit were playfully whacking each other with pillows, blissfully unaware that the days of their simple world were numbered.

Splendid Man noticed my wistful gaze and said, "It's ironic that you mentioned Thomas Wolfe, Will. Wasn't he the one who said you can't go home again?"

"Yes, and I suppose it's true," I sighed. "Even if it's someone else's home."

Then the time stream opened around us, and Turnipville was gone.

Episode Nine
Splendid Man's Splendid Street

"Cigarette, Cal?" I asked.

"No thanks," he said. "I try to keep myself down to one a day, in fear of setting a bad example for America's youth. You know, that's the third cigarette you've smoked since we flew here to my Citadel of Contemplation."

"I guess I'm nervous about the interview for that temporary job vacuuming model homes next week. I'm becoming a little too dependent on cigarettes to get me through the anxieties of daily life."

Splendid Man leaned against the can that contained Strontor, the shrunken city, and looked thoughtful. I idly wondered if Jen'Ee, my minuscule lady friend, could sense the presence of our colossal bodies, so near and yet so far away.

"It's funny you should say that," Cal said. "I feel the same way about my Splendid Powers. When I find myself wanting to smash a giant meteor or build a new orphanage at Splendid Speed not for the good of mankind but just because I'm keyed up inside, then I know something's wrong. What sort of things make you anxious, Will?"

"Oh, I don't know," I said. "Sometimes I just worry about worrying too much."

"The problem is that neither of us faces enough visceral challenges," he said. "You because of your sedentary, intellectual lifestyle, and me because things come too easily for me under the influence of Earth's argon-tinged atmosphere and lesser gravity. I think I need to get away for a while, go someplace where I can really give my all to living, without Splendid Powers."

"Such as a planet with an argon-free atmosphere like that of your native world Strontium?" I asked.

"That's right," he said. "Under an argon-free atmosphere I have no more powers than any Earthling. In fact, I know of one uninhabited argon-free planet to which my old archenemy, the blue android space criminal Cerebriac, once lured me, which would be a perfect place to get away from it all. What do you say, Will? I could get Splendid Girl to take over my patrols, and we could run up there this afternoon. We could really test ourselves against the elements. I'll bet you could use a vacation, if you're as plagued by petty anxieties as I am."

"Well, I did take a week off at Easter to visit my parents in the suburbs," I reminded him.

"But that sort of vacation just adds to your tensions, Will. We should try roughing it! There's nothing like struggling for survival on a primitive planet that's inimical to human life for a little peace of mind, believe me."

"Don't you think that's a little extreme? I know a nice state park where we can rent a rubber raft and go fishing."

"Now don't be afraid, Will. It's precisely this fear of difficulty that lies at the root of your problem. Weren't you the one who told me to read all those books by Nietzsche on life-affirmation?"

Although I knew he never meant to, Splendid Man always made me feel like a coward when I was hesitant. This time I wanted to live up to his hopes for me. I tossed my cigarette away and said, "Count me in!"

"That's fine! We'll have a great time, pal!" he exclaimed. "We're overdue for some time together anyway. Now you wait here while I salvage some plates of an old battleship I recently noticed at the bottom of the Atlantic Ocean, from which I can fashion a space vessel."

"Take your time," I said.

He flashed away. I watched in fascination on a handy monitor screen as he dove to the bottom of the sea, transformed the old metal plates at Splendid Speed into a spaceship in the shape of a giant light bulb, then welded them together with the heat setting of his Splendid Vision. Next he zipped back to land, probing the junkyards of every nation with his telescopic vision in search of all the parts he needed for his hyperspeed engine. Finally, he zoomed into outer space, where he collected elements unknown on Earth with which to power his ultrascientific craft.

Cal suddenly reappeared at my side. "The spaceship will lower us onto the argon-free planet," he explained, "then return to orbit on robot controls until I summon it back with the signal device in my belt. You'd better bring a book to read. Make it a long one."

Splendid Man took his copy of *The Decline of Pleasure* by Walter Kerr, which I had recommended, and stuffed it into the secret pouch of his cape. I went through his library and picked out *Deliverance*, which I had been meaning to reread anyway.

While I sat in the ship, Splendid Man carried it into orbit and launched it by his own power. Then he joined me in the cockpit and piloted it by its futuristic controls.

"We'll be going faster than light in just a jiffy."

"You know, until I met you," I said, "I was always under the impression that the speed of light was an absolute."

"That was Albert Einstein's idea," he said. "I've always wished I could have talked to Albert about that, but fate decreed against it."

"Couldn't you go back in time and talk to him?" I asked.

"You know how I hate to change the course of history, Will. Besides, whenever I have dropped in on him during my trips to the past, we've always found ourselves talking about religion or politics or roller derby, which he loved dearly, until it was time for him to go to bed."

I looked out the window and thought about the universe. I groped for a cigarette but my coat pocket was empty. Then I remembered.

"Er...Cal," I said. "I don't suppose we could go back for a minute, could we?"

"But, Will, we're halfway across the galaxy already. Did you forget something?"

"I'm afraid I left my cigarettes in your intergalactic menagerie."

"Oh, my," he said. "I hope the rare Rigelian Paper-Eaters don't get into them. If they do, I'll just give you the fifty cents for a new pack."

"It's more like eighty cents now, Cal."

"Great Amundsen!" he said.

"But don't worry about the money. It's just the idea of a vacation without cigarettes that upsets me."

"Surely you can just tell yourself not to crave them," he said. "That's what I do."

"Well then, you have more will than I," I said.

Cal frowned. "Was that a pun on your name, Will?"

"It wasn't meant to be."

He nodded. "I never know when you're making one of your subtle jokes. Look, Will! There's our planet!"

The ship slowed down as it entered the atmosphere of the third planet circling a medium-sized star. Below us, vast waterless deserts stretched in every direction. The spaceship landed itself in the midst of them.

"This will really be an adventure!" beamed Splendid Man as he swung through the escape hatch eagerly. "It's like your first trip as a boy scout, isn't it, Will?"

I looked out at the arid wasteland surrounding us. "I never joined the scouts," I said.

"I've always considered them an excellent way of instilling responsibility in Earthly youngsters," he said. "Look, pal! This looks like a rain-wash in the rocks. It should lead us to a water hole."

"Aren't we going to bring any food?" I asked, climbing out of the hatch.

"But Will, that would defeat the whole purpose!"

Suddenly the spaceship shot into the sky with a roar. I don't think I've ever felt as desolate as I did at that moment.

Cal hummed merrily as we trekked across the blazing desert. He kept feeling his forehead and smiling to himself, evidently pleased to find himself perspiring, which would be impossible for him while invulnerable under an argon-tinged atmosphere.

Suddenly he cried out, "Water!"

Ahead of us lay a murky water hole with stubby tree-like vegetation around it.

"We'll camp here tonight," he said. "You gather firewood, while I go see what I can do about dinner."

Gathering wood was hot work, and I soon had to sit and rest. I had reached for my cigarettes before I remembered they weren't there. Fortunately, I thought, we would only be here for the weekend, since Cal knew I would have to report to the custodial service Monday morning and would never want me to be late for a chance at a new job.

When I returned to the pond with my armload of sticks, I found that Cal had beached a giant eel, as long and thick as the cables of the Golden Gate Bridge. They were both dripping wet.

"Will!" he called exuberantly. "You sure missed an adventure! You had hardly left when a giant sand spider attacked me. Fortunately, I led it into the water, where our thrashings attracted this giant eel. The eel seized me in its coils and the spider attacked it, whereupon the eel killed the spider but gradually expired from the spider venom. Luckily, I was able to grab two reeds, one for inhaling and one for exhaling, and thereby survive through the principle of snorkeling when the eel dragged me under water."

"That was pretty resourceful of you," I said.

"And now we have dinner for tonight!"

I looked at the slimy eel in revulsion. "You mean this?"

"Of course, Will. Both Italy and Japan have long traditions of using the eel in cuisine and, as you no doubt know from your reading, jellied eels remain a popular delicacy of the English working class. We'll just have to roast ours on an open wood fire!"

"I don't have any matches," I said. "And I'm afraid I left my lighter with my cigarettes in your intergalactic menagerie."

"Oh, dear," he said. "I hope the Denebian Butane Beasts don't get to it. Was it a disposable lighter?"

"That doesn't matter," I said. "How will we light the fire?"

Cal laughed. "Don't worry about that, Will! I'll just start it with the heat setting of my...er...oh. I guess we'll have to rub two sticks together, won't we?" He looked a little crestfallen when he remembered that he had no powers, but he turned his attention to rubbing the sticks with enthusiasm. After a couple of hours he got it, and we had a nice fire.

I have to admit that the eel was remarkably tasty, but darkness brought with it a bitter cold that even the fire couldn't drive away. And to make matters worse, I started suffering from that tightening of the scrotum that affects humans in argon-free environments. I complained about it to Cal. The cold, that is.

"Let me tell you something, Will," he said. "People don't often realize what an uplifting effect the little discomforts of life, like cold and hunger and fatigue, can have on the spirit. Sometimes you can't discover the truth of yourself until you get away from the comforts of home, whether they be an apartment, a job and a car, or an argon-tinged atmosphere that grants invulnerability and Splendid Powers unparalleled in the universe. This is the life, Will! Just you and I and this barren planet!"

"I think it's getting colder," I said. "I sure could go for some hot coffee now."

"You shouldn't be a captive to your own habits, Will. You'll see. After a few weeks here, you won't give a thought to cigarettes, highballs, after-dinner coffee, money, or television programs."

"A few *weeks?*" I exclaimed. "But I have to be at an interview Monday morning!"

"Don't worry, pal. By careful manipulation of the paradoxes of faster-than-light travel, I can bring us back to your City by the Bay mere hours after we left, even if we spend a month here."

The prospect of a month without cigarettes seemed more than a little dismal, but I didn't say so. Cal was obviously looking forward to this vacation, and I knew how hard it must be for the self-appointed guardian of all mankind to take time off. The least I could do was try to share his enthusiasm. I curled up on a bed of alien moss to keep warm.

The crackling of the fire, the whisper of the wind across the water hole, and the glow of the planet's seven moons put Cal in a nostalgic mood. "I haven't felt this free since the summer vacation after seventh grade. It was the first time my foster parents, Joseph and Mary Clayton, gave me permission to leave the solar system. My science teacher had told me how awesome the cosmos was, but I didn't believe him until I saw it for myself. That was some time I had, pal."

"Sure sounds like it, pal," I said.

Splendid Man fell silent then, and I started to nod off. But then he was talking again, and I detected a rather intense earnestness in his voice.

"Will, we're good pals, aren't we?"

"The best, pal."

Then he was silent again, although I had the strong sense that he was watching me as I drifted into sleep.

My first thought the next morning, as I uncurled myself painfully from the ground, was that without coffee I was going to have to splash a lot of water on my face to wake myself up. Which made for something of a disappointment when I stood up to find that our pond was gone. There was only a dry hole in the desert before us.

"Good morning, Will," said Cal. "You may have noticed that the pond is gone."

"Yes," I said. "What happened?"

"Look up there." In the direction he pointed I saw an odd, translucent sphere drifting through the air. "My guess is that that balloon creature is the culprit who soaked up the water during the night. Unless we get it to return some of it, our vacation may by cut short by thirst."

"How will we make it give up the water?"

"Why, I'll just fly up and…er…that's a good question, pal," he said. Then a vast shadow crossed us and we looked up to see a gigantic vulture over our heads. "There's our answer," said Cal, and he commenced chucking rocks at the enormous bird. "Throw me the SOS Comb with which you summon me in emergencies, would you, pal?" he asked.

I did, and just as he caught it, the massive vulture swooped down and seized him in its huge talons. They vanished into the sky. To see Cal in such dire straits and be so helpless myself filled me with anxiety, and I groped for the cigarette pack in my empty pocket. I wondered if anything grew on this planet that I could smoke to calm my nerves.

Shortly, the balloon creature drifted back overhead and poured half its water out in a mighty gush. Then Splendid Man slid from its back and, holding his cape above his head like a parachute, splashed down softly in the half-filled water hole. I helped him out of the water and discovered red dye on my hands.

"Oh, I'm sorry," he said. "I forgot that in an argon-free environment the Strontiumese fabric of my uniform is no longer invulnerable to water and the colors run. Here's your SOS Comb. I knew that the ultrasonic signal it emits when vibrated, which is inaudible to the human ear but clear to animals and the Splendid-Powered survivors of Strontium, would startle the vulture into dropping me. I timed it so that I dropped onto the balloon creature and was able to guide it back here equestrian-style. Thanks for the help."

"Any time, pal," I said. "But how did you get the balloon creature to give us back half the water?"

"Well...er...at first I tried speaking to it in its own language, until I realized that I no longer possess the power of Splendid Recall and can only speak English, Strontiumese, and a little high-school French. Fortunately, it had picked up a little English in its interstellar travels in search of water, and I could make myself understood."

"You do very well without your Splendid Powers," I said.

He shook his head. "It's frustrating, Will. I seem to keep forgetting that I don't have any powers. I'd hate to think I've become that dependent on them."

"Don't worry about it," I said. "We just need a change of scenery. Maybe someplace with actual shade or shelter. Let's do a little exploring before the day heats up too much."

"I don't know. I feel listless this morning."

"That's probably because you haven't had anything to eat yet," I said. "I know I always get grumpy if I have to exert myself before I have a good breakfast."

He looked at me. "You mean the needs of my body can have that much influence on my mood? Great Strontium, Will! I hope that doesn't make me an unpleasant companion for you on your vacation."

"I'm sure it won't. Let's just have some more eel and take our minds off our worries. Feel your cheeks, pal. It looks like you're growing some whiskers."

"That's right! In an argon-free atmosphere, my hair and nails grow just as Earthlings' do! I'll have to remember to shave before we go, since my facial hairs will become invulnerable and unshaveable once we leave this argon-free planet."

"Have you ever considered growing a beard?"

He looked at his reflection in the water. "I don't think it suits my image."

"I think you'd look rather dashing," I said, serving him some eel with a Kleenex for a napkin.

"Do you think so?" he asked, giving me a long look. Then he shook his head. "A beard is fine for someone in the arts like yourself, Will. But I want to present an image of stability and upright morality to the world. I don't mean to sound sanctimonious, but I do try to set an example."

"You represent a standard for which we all can strive," I said. "But so did Abraham Lincoln, and look how his credibility was enhanced by a beard."

He mulled that over for a while. "That's true," he admitted. "But Lincoln did his good work through his powers of thought and statecraft, not Splendid Strength, Flight, and Vision. Far be it from me ever to criticize one of America's greatest presidents, but he and I have different public images to maintain."

"You might consider a goatee and a mustache," I said. "You'd cut quite a romantic figure."

He studied his face in the reflection for a long time. "No," he said at last. "I'd look too much like Errol Flynn. No one would take me seriously."

For the rest of the day we looked for odd alien life forms in the creek that dribbled down into the water hole. I'll admit it wasn't my favorite way to spend a day, compared to, say, stealing glances at a beautiful woman over a snifter of Calvados or curling up with a great novel while the fog flowed past my windows or even doing my laundry at the Rinse-A-Rama. But it did me good to see Splendid Man looking so relaxed. I didn't even mind so much when we sat down once again to a dinner of roasted giant eel.

"Say, pal," he said. "Thanks for today."

"Nothing to thank me for, pal," I said.

"You were very supportive of me when I was fretting about my dependence on my powers. Not just any pal would do that."

"Gosh, after all the times you've listened to me pour out my stupid little problems and tried to help me with my…"

"We're more than just literary friends, aren't we, Will? I mean, we care about each other. As people."

"Of course we do."

"Will…"

"Yeah, Cal?"

He was silent for a long moment. Again the darkness had settled around us, a soft wind made the fire dance, and the moons mounted one after another over the horizon. Cal was more pensive than I'd ever seen him.

"Will, there's something I've been meaning to tell you about myself for quite some time now, and this setting, on a planet countless light years from home, far from the associations and habits of thought fostered by the familiar, seems like the perfect time." He licked his lips nervously. "Tell me, Will, doesn't it feel wrong to you that good pals should have secrets from each other?"

"Secrets?" I asked. "Wait! Let me guess! You've finally decided to pop the question to Pepper!"

The light from the fire wasn't very bright, but I thought I saw a look of annoyance cross his face.

"No, that's not quite it, Will," he said after a while. "But I'm glad you brought up Pepper. Remember our double date?"

Oh, boy! How could I forget such a disaster?"

"Do you remember the things Pepper said that night?"

I thought back over that evening, and I remembered the nonsense she'd spouted about his sexual orientation, but I knew that couldn't be what he meant. Cal would know as well as anyone that Pepper, in an effort to shore up her womanly vanity, had been desperately seeking a rationale for why Splendid Man had yet to marry her. Then it came to me.

"Sure," I said. "She was wondering why Ken Clayton is never around when Splendid Man shows up. Good old Pepper!"

Splendid Man started tapping his fingers against his leg, a nervous habit he'd never displayed before. He cleared his throat a couple of times and said, "Yes, that she did. Let's try a different tack for a while. Have you ever noticed anything a little...well...unusual about my Citadel of Contemplation? When you take into account that I'm a bachelor, that is?"

"Well, I'm not clear on how the bachelor part fits in, but that Self-Absorption Beast from Betelgeuse in your intergalactic menagerie is pretty darn unusual."

Cal took a deep breath and let it out very slowly. "Notice anything else, Will?" he asked in a strangely tight voice. Whatever the secret was that he wanted to share with me must really have been preying on his mind.

"Now that you mention it, I have noticed that you're an extremely talented interior decorator. In fact, I've been meaning to ask you, would you categorize this talent as another of your Splendid Powers?"

The tattoo he was beating with his fingertips increased in tempo. "Did you notice my Erté statuettes, Will?"

"Sure. I got to know his work well when I had that temporary sales job in that gallery on Fisherman's Wharf."

"Do you know much about Erté himself?" he persisted, and his fingertips went tap tap tap tap tap.

"A bit. Let's see, I know he was a big-time fashion and stage designer in the twenties and thirties. And then he did fashion drawings for *Harper's Bazaar* for quite a long while. In fact, he had a big resurgence just recently, doing stage designs for *Stardust* and producing a bunch of..."

"No, Will. I meant, what do you know about his personal life?"

"Oh. Well, I know he was born in Russia, and that his father wanted him to follow a career in the military. But he wouldn't have any of it, and in the nineteen-teens sometime he moved to Paris where he started designing...."

"NO!" Cal shouted so loud that had he still possessed his Splendid Lung Power he would have blown out my eardrums.

"What th—?" I said.

He cleared his throat again, loudly and protractedly. "Sorry," he said, "I felt a sneeze coming on. Now, Will," he continued, "try to keep up with your old pal here. Okay?"

"Sure thing, Cal."

"Remember our trip to Turnipville?"

"How could I forget?" I said. "My beard still hasn't filled in." But I was thinking that Splendid Man's secret must be awfully convoluted to involve so many people, places, and things.

"Remember our little talk before we left your apartment? When I told you about my days growing up in Turnipville? About the alienation I felt, the burden of shouldering so great a secret?"

"Sure I remember, pal."

"Well, just ask yourself, Will. What do you think I was driving at? When I talked about how I didn't fit in, and how I felt different from other boys?"

"I'm sorry, Cal, but isn't that a little obvious? You had to conceal the fact that you were an alien from outer space. I get it already. It was stressful."

Splendid Man was staring at me incredulously. Then he was on his feet and pacing back and forth so vigorously that even bereft of his Splendid Tread I thought he was going to dig a trench in the sand.

"Will," he said.

"Yes, pal?"

"Will!" he cried.

"I'm right here, Cal."

"That's not what I was driving at!" he said.

"Sorry, Cal."

He took another deep breath to steady himself. "Try to keep up with me now. Okay, pal?"

"I'm trying, pal."

"That's all I ask, pal. Just that you try to keep up with your old pal here."

"I'm right there with you, pal."

"Now, tell me, do you remember the evening we spent at stately Brewster manor?"

"Sure I do, Cal."

"And you remember how Wyatt was talking to you about subtexts?"

"Of course. Are you saying there was a subtext to our conversation that night?"

"That's it, Will! I'm starting to feel you're with me now, pal! Let's see if we can stay on the same page just a little longer. Okay, pal?"

"You got it, pal!"

"Okay. Great. Now, do you remember when we were driving back to Brewster Manor following our little adventure?"

"You bet I do!"

"That's fine, Will. Just fine. And now we're getting to the nitty-gritty. Remember when you asked us if we didn't think Batwoman was a doll? And Wyatt started to say something, but then he pulled up short, and instead he said…"

"Sure, I remember," I said. "I remember it occurred to me at the time that…"

Then it hit me. And left me stunned.

"You don't mean…" I asked, when I could trust my voice not to quaver. "You don't mean…you too?"

He held my eyes for a moment, then simply nodded.

I shook my head in disbelief. "Oh, jeez. Forgive me if I'm flabbergasted, Cal. Wyatt I can understand. He's got the intensity and the flamboyance. But you! I'm sorry, but I just can't imagine you being part of that world!"

"But I am, Will."

"Wow. I mean, I'm not making any judgments or anything, but

this is really going to take some getting used to."

"I understand, Will."

"Man. Then all these years, while you've been brushing off poor Pepper...you've been sleeping around with the likes of Batwoman and Venus Flytrap and whatever other promiscuous villainesses have thrown themselves at you!"

Splendid Man's hands flew to his head. He started to squeeze. He squeezed so hard I thought his brains were going to pop out of his ears. He was breathing hard.

"Are you okay, pal?"

His fingers gradually relaxed. His breath began to quiet. "Believe it or not, pal," he finally said, "that's *not* what I meant."

"Then I guess I just don't get it, pal," I said.

He threw himself on his bed of moss. He stared at the stars for a spell then rolled over on his side, his back to me. "Goodnight, Will," he said.

"But, pal," I said, "aren't you going to unburden yourself of that secret?"

"Tomorrow, Will," he said, his voice sounding awfully weary. "I'll tell you about it tomorrow."

It took me a long time to fall asleep, troubled as I was by the question of what secret could be bothering my pal so much that he was apparently afraid to tell even me. Then I reminded myself that I knew Splendid Man, as only one true friend can know another, and that nothing I learned could change my opinion of him. With that thought to comfort me, and with the septuple moons following their criss-crossing paths through the sky above me, I surrendered to slumber at last.

The next morning I awoke to find myself alone. Sitting up abruptly, I saw Splendid Man some distance away, gazing out over the desolate wastes of our planet.

"Eel, pal?" I said. I'd wrapped a hunk of meat in Kleenex and carried it to him. He took it with a quiet smile. "I'm getting to like this stuff," I said, tossing aside the Kleenex. "Maybe we should make jerky to take home with us."

"I'm glad you enjoy it," he said. "But please don't throw your

Kleenex on the ground. No offense, pal, but as visitors to this planet we can't be so presumptuous as to litter it. You know what they say. Take only memories, leave only footprints."

"Of course, you're right, pal," I said. "I'll go get it."

"Don't bother," he said. "With my Splendid Breath I can...Darn it! There I go again! I've made such a habit of using my powers for everything that I can't remember when I don't have them!"

"That's normal, Cal. I myself keep reaching in my pocket, expecting to find cigarettes there."

He got up and retrieved my discarded Kleenex. I could tell something was weighing on his mind. A lot of people think Splendid Man never shows his worries on his face. But they don't know him like I do.

"A little tobacco would be nice right now, wouldn't it?" he asked suddenly.

"It sure would," I said. "And a little coffee after breakfast, to perk us up for the day."

He nodded. "Want to hear my secret now, pal?"

"I'm all ears."

He paused for a moment. Then he said, "I'm not enjoying this adventure. That's what I didn't want to admit. I thought I could do without my Splendid Stunts, but now I find I really miss soaring into outer space and breaking the time barrier and battling such foes as Giganto the Splendid Mandrill, the Hideous Thing from 1,000,000 A.D., and Plasto, the Man with the Strontiumite Spleen. Even the little things: scanning the earth with the telescopic setting of my Splendid Vision, diverting tidal waves, adding bizarre specimens to the intergalactic menagerie in my lunar Citadel of Contemplation. And I miss my other friends, and my things. That's why I kept bringing them up last night. I hope you're not disappointed in me, Will."

I smiled and said, "I'll tell you what, Cal. Until I find the strength to give up smoking, I won't criticize you for being unable to give up your Splendid Powers."

"It's a deal," he grinned. "Say, Will? Would you be

disappointed if we went home early? We could visit a few nice argon-tinged planets on the way back."

"That's fine with me," I said, "if that's what you want. Maybe we can catch a movie back in the city."

"That sounds nice and familiar." Then, thoughtfully, he added, "I hope I didn't make you anxious last night with all my talk of a 'big secret.'"

"Don't worry about it, Cal. I knew it couldn't possibly be anything that would change my opinion of you."

He put his hand on my shoulder and fixed me with a strange look that seemed to mingle affection, amusement, and dismay all at once. "You have quite an unshakeable image of your old pal Splendid Man, don't you, Will?"

"It's a great image," I said. "As pure and strong as my image of Abe Lincoln."

"Well," Cal chuckled, "he and I both have beards!"

And with that, he signaled for the spaceship.

Episode Ten
All Your Favorite Heroes

My shift at my latest temporary job was almost over when Splendid Man dropped in to browse. I was shelving paperback fiction. I'd introduced him to my coworkers before, but I could see by the way they blushed and stuttered when he greeted them by name that they were still in awe of him. The few customers in the shop stared at him slack-jawed. He didn't particularly seem to notice.

"If you see anything you think I should read, let me know, Will."

"Will do," I said. "But could you help me here? I'd like to get this whole box up on the shelves by six, so that I can leave on time."

"Of course, pal. Why Will! These books don't seem to be in very good order!"

"My manager says it's not cost effective to spend time alphabetizing paperbacks," I said, "what with the tiny profit we make on each. She just wants authors whose names start with the same letter more or less near each other."

"But Will, that just isn't right!" he cried. "For people on modest incomes, a used paperback may be the only way to own quality fiction! Why should someone of limited means have to spend time digging through giant stacks of James Clavell and Taylor Caldwell to find that one elusive...um..."

"Evan S. Connell?"

"Exactly! Evan S. Connell! When someone better-heeled can snag it instantly from the meticulously alphabetized hardbacks? I tell you, Will, it's an injustice. Not a malicious one, of course, knowing your kindly manager, but the result is the same."

"I appreciate your outrage, pal, really I do," I said. "But the reality of minimum-wage life is that you have to buy into a lot of injustice just to get by."

Without a word, Splendid Man exploded into action, whizzing past me, behind me, and all around me, countless times a second. The whole paperback fiction section became a red and gold blur. Before my eyes, the books on the shelves assumed a perfect alphabetical order.

"There," said Splendid Man beaming, separating one last Frank Yerby novel from the Emile Zolas.

The whole staff clapped their hands exuberantly.

"Thanks, Cal," I said. "And I wish I could tell you that your splendid efforts made a real difference. But the sad truth is, by tomorrow afternoon the customers will have reduced this whole section back to its accustomed chaos."

He frowned thoughtfully at that. "You know, Will, that's often the way life is. No matter how much good you may achieve, time will undo you. I shudder to think how many times I've put my archenemy Pox Pascal behind bars, only to see him escape again. Maybe I should fly over this bookstore periodically and check the shelves with the combined X-ray and telescopic settings of my Splendid Vision to see if anything needs reorganizing."

"Don't worry about it," I said, patting his arm. "You have enough to do as it is without watching over bookstores. Come on. Let's go out for a drink."

At the counter, as I filled out my time card, I pointed out a rare copy of Philip Wylie's *Gladiator*, priced at $40.00.

"There's a book you might find interesting," I said, "if you ever have a little extra money to throw around."

He scrutinized the cover. "You know, I've never cared for science fiction. It's a little too fantastic for my taste."

Just then, his chest emblem emitted a high-pitched whistle. Customers looked around to see where it was coming from. Cal signaled me, and we stepped outside. As usual, people pointed and gawked and said, "Splendid Man! Splendid Man!"

"That was my emergency signal from the North American

Alliance for Meetness," he said.

"I guess that means tonight's off," I said glumly.

"I hate to do that to you, pal. Maybe it'll be a short case and we can still get together for a little coffee and dessert in the evening. Of course, if it's a long case…I'll tell you what, Will. How would you like to come to an NAAFM meeting?"

"And meet the most famous and powerful of the world's Splendid Heroes in their legendary sanctuary? I'd like that fine."

"I'm sure the other fellows and gals would be happy to meet you," he said. "After all, you introduced me to your coworkers here at the bookstore. The least I can do is introduce you to my fellow defenders of mankind. Let me wrap you in my cape to protect you from the winds during our Splendid Speed flight, and I'll fly you to the Alliance's secret sanctuary. I can't allow you to see the actual location…"

"Of course not," I said. "There are too many enemies of the North American Alliance for Meetness who'd stop at nothing to trick or coerce that information from me. But there's one thing you've got to tell me, Cal."

"What's that, Will?"

"What the hell does '*meetness*' mean?"

"It means that which is suitable, or fair."

"I see," I said. "I imagine it could also mean that which is just. As in justice."

"That's finessing it a bit," he said, "but yes, it could be made to mean that."

"I get it now," I said. "But tell me, couldn't you guys have come up with something better? Or at least something that yielded a catchier acronym than NAAFM?"

He chuckled. "Actually, there's a pretty funny story there, Will. You've read about Condor's exploits in the comics, haven't you?"

"Of course. A native of the planet Altoona who, with his beauteous wife Condora, came to Earth to study our agricultural methods, only to discover that he liked crime-fighting better."

"That's him. As you no doubt know, the advanced science of

Altoona developed a device called the Retain-a-Con that enables its user to absorb instantly the totality of any planet's knowledge. Well, when using this device to learn our language, Condor didn't just learn English, he learned every English word that's ever been part of the language, including words that have long passed from common usage."

"I get it," I said. "The name was Condor's idea."

"Right. And he was so proud of himself—you know how puffed-up people get when they learn to say even a few words in another language—that nobody had the heart to tell him how stupid it sounds."

We laughed.

"Over time, though, we've all grown rather fond of it," he added. "Pretty soon we were all aspiring to meetness in everything we did. Are you ready to go, Will?"

"As I'll ever be."

Without further ado, Splendid Man wrapped me in his cape and we flashed into the sky. When he drew the cape from my eyes I saw that we were over a desert landscape of buttes and tall rocks, and there ahead of us, set into a red cliff, loomed the legendary doors of the great headquarters building. From every quarter of the sky, other heroes sped to answer the emergency signal: Northern Light, flying by the auroral might of his mystic medallion; Va Va Voom, piloting her visible robot plane, devised by the ultrascientific amazons of time-tossed Lesbo Island; and Quickie, a mere verdant streak of Splendid Speed across the earth. I imagined others would be arriving shortly: Condor and Condora by the power of the flight belts from their native Altoona, a planet orbiting Sirius; Crimson Spear in his angry red Spear Plane; and Joe Ethel, Merman, with the aid of some strange water beast. My spirit soared at the thought of all my favorite heroes in one sanctuary.

Northern Light, Quickie, and Va Va Voom were already at the long NAAFM meeting table when we entered. As Splendid Man prepared to introduce me to the others, brown-skinned Carlos Osvaldo Jones (pronounced "Ho-ness"), Manhunter from Mexico, flew through the door. Then a beam of light suddenly appeared overhead, an orange and black dot in its midst. The dot soon separated itself from the beam and rapidly grew into a little man. It was the Quark, that mighty mite, arriving by his favorite means of transportation, a beam of light, riding it sometimes as a wave, sometimes as a particle.

"Well, Splendid Man, who's your friend?" he piped in his tiny voice, when he had enlarged to his full six-inch size.

"Everyone, this is my friend Will Jones," said Splendid Man. I was pleased to see all their faces light up in recognition of the name. Splendid Man introduced me to each of the heroes in turn. Before he could finish, Condor and Condora arrived, followed quickly by Stretchy McCutchy and finally Joe Ethel, Merman. The heroes and I exchanged nods, but the tense mood was not conducive to conversation.

Condor asked, "Who called this emergency colloquium?"

"I did," said Catman, appearing suddenly from one of the vast monitor rooms. He tossed me a little salute in greeting, which I returned with a grin. "Our old nemesis Q.U.E. Sera-Sera, the twisted scientific genius whose name has always filled him with a fascination for the workings of fate, has launched another attack on the earth with his futuristic weapons."

"He's reckoned without the North American Alliance for Meetness," said Splendid Man. "We've stopped him before and we'll stop him again."

"To be sure," Catman said dryly. "Va Va Voom and Stretchy McCutchy, you will fly to Guadalajara, Mexico, where a giant ray-blaster is threatening to set off dangerous earthquake faults. Meanwhile, Mexican Manhunter and Joe Ethel, Merman, will speed to the Island of the Four Mountains in the North Pacific, where a giant robot is wreaking havoc on the peaceful populace. Crimson Spear and…where is Crimson Spear?"

"He didn't show up," said Quickie.

"That son of a bitch," said Northern Light.

"We'll have time for personal differences later," said Catman. "We'll simply have to do without the Scarlet Spear Chucker."

"We should be getting good at it by now," grumbled Northern Light.

"Ignoring the emergency signal is simply not meet!" huffed Va Va Voom.

Catman continued, "Condor and Condora, fly to your orbiting Altoonan scientific station and see what your Retain-a-Con can tell us about Q.U.E. Sera-Sera."

"Momentaneously," Condor said, and he and his mate departed with a rustle of their mighty wings.

"Splendid Man and I will beard Q.U.E. Sera-Sera in his lair high in the Rockies of Wyoming," said Catman. "Quark, Northern Light, and Quickie, you will guard our secret sanctuary in case our villainous opponent launches an assault on our very sanctum sanctorum." He caught my eye and winked. "And watch over our friend William here."

"Oh, don't trouble about me," I said.

"Nonsense," said Quickie. "It's no trouble at all."

The others were gone in an instant, all grinning and flexing their muscles. Quickie, the swiftest man alive, the Quark, that gossamer gumshoe, and the auroral acrobat, Northern Light, were all left at the table with me.

"Say guys," I said. "Can one of you explain why everybody always refers to Va Va Voom's plane as *visible*? I mean, I don't get it. It if was *invisible*, then it would make sense. You would say, 'Look, there's Va Va Voom in her invisible plane.' You know? Because it would be conspicuous to see a woman seeming to float in mid-air as she pilots an invisible plane. But as it is, the plane looks like any other plane, so what is it about its *visibility* that makes it noteworthy?"

They all looked blankly at each other.

"That's funny," Quickie said. "Now that Will's mentioned it, I realize that I don't have the slightest idea. You, Quark? NL?"

Quark shook his little head. "Beats me all hollow."

"Don't know," Northern Light said. "And don't rightly know that I give a crap."

That settled, apparently, Quickie turned to me and said, "So,

Will. Splendid Man tells us that you're a novelist."

"Well," I said modestly, "I do like to write."

"You know, I've never been much for novels," said Quickie. "Maybe I should try a few. I mostly read nonfiction. Medical reports and so on. You see, in my secret identity I'm an X-ray technician."

"I've always enjoyed collecting odd facts," chirped that six-inch savage, the Quark. "I find they help me on my adventures. Did you know that the stone opal is primarily composed of water?"

"Uh, no, I had no idea," I said.

"You'd be amazed how useful such information can be when battling costumed villains," twittered the teeny tussler. "I like novels that inform me. Have you ever read Michener?"

"He's, uh, very informative," I said.

"I've always thought that I might want to write a novel someday," said Quickie, leaning back thoughtfully. I was struck by the slowness of his movements, quite ironic for the speediest hero on Earth and most likely a source of many droll misunderstandings in his secret identity. "I guess I just wouldn't know how. They say everybody has a novel in him, though. Don't they? The story of his own life, I mean?"

"You see, I'm a popular-science writer in my secret identity," cheeped the lilliputian lawman. "I like historical novels, if they're well researched."

"Yes, research is very important," I agreed.

"Damn that Crimson Spear," said Northern Light suddenly, brushing his hair back from his handsome face. "How many meetings has he missed? Ever since he got goddamned socially conscious and decided goddamned Splendid Heroes ought to be fighting goddamned slum lords, he can't be bothered to fight a *real* Splendid Villain!"

Quickie chuckled and patted Northern Light's knee condescendingly. "I agree it isn't meet that he should miss so many meetings, NL, but don't let him get under your skin. I think you two just spend too much time together. Why don't you join the conversation?"

"Sorry, Will," said Northern Light, reaching across the table to shake my hand. "I'm afraid I'm rather hard on my compatriots."

"No harder than he is on himself," said Quickie with a wink. "N.L.'s the perfectionist of our little Splendid Hero union. Still, he's been known to bend an elbow now and then in his private life."

"As a race-car driver in my secret identity, and the boyfriend of the daughter of the boss of a major auto-manufacturing corporation in Canuck City, I often find myself in a rather fast crowd," said the auroral avenger.

"Did you know that dogs can tell their masters are homeward bound even when they're still miles away?" pipped the minuscule marauder.

"You know, I've never gone much for the sports cars and debutantes and champagne life," said the sultan of speed. "I have my partner, and my home in the Midwest, very tastefully furnished. My partner had done it all in Early American, but I've been finding some lovely Art Deco pieces…"

That ferocious flea, the Quark, tittered. "I'm afraid a popular-science writer's earnings wouldn't buy me much champagne!"

Then Condor and Condora returned from their space station. Their bizarre headgear made me a little uneasy at first, but they were charming in the manner of so many cultured immigrants.

"Q.U.E. Sera-Sera's very pregnability is his dependency on weapons of the future, when Splendid Heroes do not draw the breath of life," announced Condor.

Beside me, Northern Light muttered, "Speak English, motherfucker."

"He is," I whispered.

"My auroral ass," he said.

"Haven't you fellows offered Will anything to eat or drink while he's waiting?" asked the exotic Condora.

"Well, I'm sorry about that," said Quickie. "We got to talking about books. I was telling him that I might want to write a novel myself someday. What do you think, Will? I'll tell you the story and you write it. We'll split the proceeds fifty-fifty. I guarantee you it will be a bestseller."

"Did you know that there are eighteen different animal shapes in the Animal Crackers cookie zoo?" chirruped that rowdy runt, the Quark.

Everybody ignored him.

"What sort of penny dreadfuls do you pen, Will?" asked Condor, settling his great winged form into a chair.

It took me a moment. "Just contemporary realistic novels," I said.

"I always enjoy books about scientific farming," said Condor. "Do you know Louis Bromfield?"

"We originally came from Altoona to Earth to study Earthly agricultural methods," explained Condora.

"Fascinating," I said.

"I'll bet we could get a novel out of all the times I've battled General Gelid," said Quickie. "Now there's a character! The first time we met, he used his Brrrrr Pistol to…"

"Come on, Quickie," said Northern Light with a grin. "Will doesn't want to hear your damned stories."

"How do you know he doesn't?" asked Quickie. "Will, did you know that just as intense heat creates mirages, so does intense cold create them too?"

"Hey, I didn't know that," tweeted the Quark, that boring brownie. "Now there's an odd fact I'll have to add to my collection!"

"Well, General Gelid knew it," said Quickie, tapping his skull to emphasize General Gelid's cleverness.

"Say, Will," said Northern Light, changing the subject. "How are the woman troubles?"

I was taken aback. "Well, I…er…I've got nothing to complain about at the moment…"

"Don't embarrass him now!" snapped Condora. "It isn't meet!"

"I'm not embarrassing him," said Northern Light. "I'm just confronting the facts without fear. Splendid Man's talked more about Will's girl problems than he has about his writing, and that's the truth."

"Cal's been helping me out," I said.

"Ruining your life, you mean," grinned Northern Light, and the others laughed. "Listen, I don't mean to say anything against Cal. As the self-appointed protector of mankind, he's without peer. But when it comes to the skirts…"

"Now, Northern Light!" warned Condora.

"I'll leave it at that," said Northern Light. "My point is that if you want help with the fair sex, you should talk to a Splendid Hero with a little more experience, that's all."

"Who might you be thinking of?" snickered that savage shrimp, the Quark.

"Let's get a woman's opinion," said Quickie. "Condora, how do you think Will could make himself more attractive to the girls?"

"Well, I think he's quite charming as he is, for an Earthling," said Condora. "I've always liked quiet, cultured men."

I realized again how much I hated to be seen as a quiet, cultured man, but I knew she meant well, and so I kept quiet. Suddenly, there was a heavy footfall. Va Va Voom and Stretchy McCutchy had returned.

"Just as a pistol can be made to misfire by the introduction of a foreign body," explained Va Va Voom, "so Stretchy McCutchy was easily able to jam the ray-blaster with his incredibly pliable body while I used my Lesbic strength to hold the fault together."

Va Va Voom was utterly spectacular. If you were to combine Kim Novak, Anita Ekberg, and Lynda Carter, you'd only begin to approximate her magnificence. I found myself wondering about the rumors that she liked girls.

"Did you know that the name Va Va Voom originated in the Cycladic culture of the Eastern Mediterranean 4,000 years ago?" peeped that picayune palooka, the Quark. "Ironically, it originally meant, 'She who stands supreme,' but by the 20th Century it had become just a vulgar noise men make around pretty girls."

"We're having an argument here," said Quickie. "Va Va, how do you think Will here could improve his chances with the ladies?"

"I have little to contribute," answered the fabulous feminist, "coming as I do from an ancient civilization where the advancement of science has rendered men obsolete. Still, I'd venture that there is no substitute for a well-toned musculature and a strong constitution."

Stretchy McCutchy laughed. "Except maybe a prehensile proboscis!" The stretchable sleuth extended his nose ten feet in front of him, wrapped it around a coffee cup, and drew it back to his mouth. Va Va Voom looked slightly disdainful, but I found him immediately likable.

"So, you must be the author," he said brightly.

"Well..." I began, but he chattered on.

"I love mysteries. Edgar Allan Poe, Wilkie Collins. An occasional Agatha Christie, Dorothy Sayers."

"Hammett? Chandler?" I asked.

He wrapped one attenuated limb around me. "Now you're talking literature!" he said. "To quote Ross MacDonald, 'Chandler wrote like a slumming angel. He invested the sun-blinded streets of L.A. with a romantic presence.'"

"Very good!" I said.

"You're my kind of writer, I have a feeling," he said. "Have you ever tried talking to Catman about literature?"

"We chatted a while," I said.

Stretchy McCutchy made a contorted face, but Quickie said, "Don't start in on Catman's bombastic ways, now. Say, Will, I've been giving the matter a little thought. Do you know any good how-to-write books?"

"*Elements of Style* by Strunk and White is rather basic," I said. "And *Structuring your Novel* by Meredith and Fitzgerald."

With a flash of green, he was gone through the wall.

Va Va Voom noted, "Just as a straw blown by a hurricane can penetrate an oak tree, so can Quickie, traveling at Splendid Speed, pass through solid walls."

"I see," I said.

An instant later, Quickie was back. "Sorry I took so long," he said. "There was a line, and I didn't think it'd be meet to cut in. Are these the books?"

"Those are the ones," I said.

"You aren't still thinking about writing that novel of yours, are you?" asked Stretchy McCutchy.

"Maybe you'd like to help," said Quickie. "Remember our second adventure together, when you went searching the jungles of the Amazon for Fungel, the rare vegetable whose essence gives you your Splendid Power of Elasticity?"

"And I blundered onto an invasion of Martians from that planet's distant past before its evil, ultrascientific civilization had perished?"

"And I came to help you and both our heads were shrunken by the Martian head-shrinking ray?"

"And you destroyed the Martian ray gun by windmilling your arm so swiftly that it became a buzz saw and sliced right through it?"

While the others chatted animatedly, Northern Light drew me to him discreetly with his mystic beam. "Listen, Will," he said. "You and I ought to consider a double date sometime. With my looks and daring lifestyle and innate lack of fear, and your knowledge of literature and art and…all that…well, hell, we'd be a deadly combination!"

"I'd like that," I said.

"See, believe it or not, there's a downside to being a hero," he said earnestly. "Our lives are just action, action, action. All we talk about is our archvillains and our latest miraculous comebacks from apparent annihilation. Oh, sure, sometimes we'll kick back and jaw about sports or food or the best bizarre alien vacation spots. But we never learn about the finer things in life. Ever since Splendid Man met you, he's been telling us things that just zoom over our heads. You know, I tried to read *Ulysses* and I couldn't get a damned thing out of it."

"It's a difficult book," I said.

"But women love that stuff! My girl Midge—and she's a real *girl*friend, if you know what I mean—always wants to talk about her 'Gorp' or her 'Timeless Love' or her 'Music for Lizards' or whatever the hell her book group's been reading, and what do I know about it? I've been off in the negative universe of Xaxada battling Macabro, the renegade Northern Light, or some goddamn thing."

"I can see the problem," I said.

"And let's face it, Will," he said, leaning in a little closer, "you've got to know you're wasting your time asking Splendid Man's advice in the girl department."

"Well, I don't know about…"

"I mean, you know the truth about him, right? No secrets between friends?"

I bristled a little at that. So what if Cal secretly felt more dependent on his Splendid Powers than he wanted to admit? I'd like to see the Canadian Crimebuster try tussling with an alien bubble creature without the aid of his mystic medallion!

"Don't get me wrong, I don't have any problems with it," he continued. "I mean, most of these guys I fight evil alongside of are…well, you know."

"They're splendid," I said, with more than a trace of indignation.

"Bingo," he said with a wink. "You and I know what we're talking about. Now, if we were to…"

He didn't finish his sentence, because at that moment, the Mexican Manhunter and Joe Ethel, Merman, returned from their mission, grinning broadly.

"My loyal sea creatures toppled the giant robot into the ocean!" beamed Joe Ethel, Merman.

"He splash water on me," grinned the Mexican Manhunter, "and this, how you say, it make me to have the debilitating dysentery if the water is come from north of my border. But I blow away it with my Mexican Breath!"

"Hey, Merman, could you get me a beer?" called Northern Light.

"Make it two," said Quickie. "How about you, Will? Make it three, buddy!"

Joe Ethel, Merman, stood under the special shower devised to give him the dose of water he required every seventy-three minutes and fourteen seconds, without which he would shrivel and die, and then opened the refrigerator and pulled out three Miller Lights. Just then, with a flash of red and gold, Splendid Man returned, bearing Catman in his arms. By the grin on Splendid Man's face and the sneer on Catman's, we could all tell that they had succeeded in their mission. Everyone applauded.

"Q.U.E. Sera-Sera is back in jail where he belongs," said Splendid Man. "Someday criminals will learn that it isn't meet that evil should ever triumph over good."

Catman rolled his eyes.

"Hear hear!" squeaked that spunky speck, the Quark.

"Drinks all around!" said Stretchy McCutchy.

"Hey, it's Miller Time!" said Quickie.

"Honestly, how can you drink that swill?" asked Condora.

Northern Light popped the top of his can and raised his beer in a toast. "Here's to all the bastards who give us the chance to be heroes."

"You all seem very cheerful," said Splendid Man. "Are you enjoying Will's company?"

"Hell, I'm having a great time!" said Northern Light. "Will's a great listener!"

He and I clinked beer cans in a salute.

"Since we were all so successful," said Quickie, "does anyone feel like a ball game? There must be a good one somewhere in this country tonight."

"There's a Giant-Dodger game in Los Angeles," I said.

"I would like to see this young Fernando Valenzuela in action," said Splendid Man. "I always appreciate excellence in our young folks."

"Baseball is for pussies," said Northern Light. "But hell, it's not hockey season!"

"For me, I love it the *fútbol*!" grinned the Mexican Manhunter.

"How tedious," said Condora.

"Some integrants of Earth's culture still maze us," said Condor.

"Jesus Christ," Northern Light muttered, then in full voice said, "Before we run off to a game, I'd like to suggest something. As you know, we used to have a teen mascot named Clapper Otto. We made him an honorary member in recognition of the assistance he gave us on our early mission against Horso, the giant hypnotic seahorse."

"Good old Clapper," said Quickie wistfully. "I still remember how he'd clap his hands and say something in that preposterous hep-cat slang of his. 'Beam me in, Daddy-O, 'cause this cat's ears are itchin' to blow.' Or something like that."

"But now the changing times have turned Clapper into a grim creature of the night driven only by vengeance," said Va Va Voom. "He's even taken to speaking in proper English. It isn't meet!"

"Personally, I think it's high time that we had another mascot," said Northern Light.

"Well, what a nice idea," said Splendid Man. "I move that Will Jones be elected an honorary member of the North American Alliance for Meetness!"

That huge brown Mexican, C. O. Jones, punched me in the arm and said, "Yeah sure, I vote for second that! *¿Quién sabe?* Maybe Will and I could to be related!"

Everyone laughed. And then, when the vote was taken, I was unanimously elected into that noblest and most powerful of clubs on earth, albeit with the stupidest name, the North American Alliance for Meetness.

I'm not ashamed to say that there were tears in my eyes. Even if it wasn't meet.

Episode Eleven
Splendid Girl's True Love

I was hiking around the rocks at Land's End, above the Golden Gate, ignoring the danger signs. Ever since my vacation with Cal to that argon-free planet, I'd been criticizing myself for being too physically timid. This was a chance to prove to myself that I could do more than stroll along a paved path, and in a way that I figured couldn't get me into real trouble. Man, was I wrong about that last part! A small wave broke over the rocks around me, and the next thing I knew I was plunging into the ocean.

"Help!" I cried as I went down. "I don't know how long I can…glub…"

I'd always meant to ask Cal if the SOS Comb worked underwater. I figured I'd be finding out now. Within instants, a familiar red and gold blur swooped down and saved me.

When my feet were back on dry land I said, "Thanks, pal! For once I had a real emergency!" But to my surprise I found myself addressing a dainty teenage girl in a costume like Splendid Man's, but with a very short skirt instead of tights. "Oh," I said. "You must be Cal's cousin Kar'En."

Surprisingly, Splendid Girl only nodded shyly and blushed.

"I guess the SOS Comb did work," I said.

"What do you mean?" she asked.

"Didn't you respond to my signal?"

"No. Pura Poseidonis, the mermaid from Lemuria, contacted me telepathically when she saw you were in trouble."

"Thanks for saving my life," I said, "and thank Pura for me the next time you see her. I'm Will Jones, by the way."

Splendid Girl blushed again. And as she did so, I was struck by her loveliness. I don't usually get worked up over teenage girls—

even that sizzling redhead Patti Pert was more of a promising rough draft than a satisfying final product—but Kar'En was different somehow. I wondered if it was the trace quantity of argon in our atmosphere that put the strawberry in her lips, the rose-bloom in her cheeks, and the glacial blueness in her huge eyes that hinted at a maturity beyond her years. Was it Earth's lesser gravity that lent such grace to her lithesome limbs, such buoyancy and self-assuredness to her posture? And while her looks did have something of the plastic cuteness portrayed in the comics—a dollop of Shelley Fabares, a smidgen of Sandra Dee—there were also present the exoticism of her Strontiumese ancestry and the strength of character gained from years as Splendid Man's helper. And those red boots! Lord have mercy!

"Well," she said suddenly, perhaps made uncomfortable by my scrutiny, "I should fly you home so you can change out of those wet clothes."

She seemed a little embarrassed while trying to figure out how to carry me for our flight.

"Why don't I just put my arm around your waist?" I offered.

"I...I guess that would be okay," she stammered meekly, but she made no move to approach me.

Finally I stepped up to her and said, "Which side is better for you, your left or your right?"

"It doesn't matter," she said. "Strontiumese natives are ambidextrous in an argon-tinged atmosphere."

We took to the skies. "I live just over there," I said, pointing.

"I know," she said, but quickly added, "Er...Splendid Man told me in case I ever had to rescue you, or something."

We flew the rest of the way in silence. I would have loved to make conversation, but I discovered that holding on to her, rather than being carried, was a lot harder than I'd anticipated, and I was struck dumb from terror of losing my grip and plummeting to my death. After what seemed an eternity, she set me down outside the gate.

"Would you like to come in for some coffee?" I said, when my knees had stopped shaking.

"I...er...I'd like to," she said. "But my foster mother always tells me never to go into a strange man's apartment."

"Would you care to wait while I change and then go out for a cup?" I asked.

She glanced down at her feet and said, "I'd love to."

As I changed into dry jeans, a t-shirt, and my one decent jacket, a surge of excitement electrified me. I couldn't get those big liquidy eyes out of my mind. And those little boots!

When I returned to the street I was crushed to find Splendid Girl gone. Where she had been stood a gangly teenage girl with mousy brown pigtails. She was dressed in a plaid skirt, a nondescript white blouse, bobby socks, and Mary Janes.

"Excuse me, young lady," I said, scanning the sky. "Have you seen Splendid Girl near here?"

"Don't you recognize me?" she asked.

I looked at her and reviewed the faces of all the neighbors and the various coworkers I'd had at all my temporary jobs, including my current one at the sofa-bed showroom, but to no avail. "I'm afraid not," I said.

"It's me!" she exclaimed. "Splendid Girl, in my secret identity as Peggy Pearl Perkins!"

"My God," I said. "Your disguise is...remarkable."

She smiled, pleased, but she didn't realize I hadn't meant it as a compliment. I hadn't pictured myself walking the streets with this prematurely frumpy adolescent, but with a golden-haired Splendid Heroine whose skimpy, skin-tight uniform barely covered her marvelous...

Then I caught myself. What would Cal think if he knew of the impure thoughts I'd nearly had for his little cousin? I decided to make the best of the situation. I put out my arm and Peggy bashfully took it. On the way to a cafe in my neighborhood I asked, "How is it that you came to my aid instead of your Splendid Cousin?"

"He couldn't come," Peggy explained, "because he's busy defending a parallel Earth from an interdimensional menace from outer space. He asked me to watch over you and his pals Pepper and Bobby and Oliver Hazard Black in his absence."

I chose the cafe purposely to make an impression. It was one of those picturesque Italian places that San Francisco used to be famous for but are so hard to find anymore, with opera on the jukebox, cannoli in the display case, and swarthy fellows in white neckties and fedoras huddled in the booths talking about whatever it is Italians talk about. Frank Sinatra records, I suppose, or the Bocce Ball standings. The only patron who did not seem so quaintly ethnic was an elderly gentleman in a conservative suit who read the newspaper at the counter.

When the stocky waitress with the mustache tromped over to us, I ordered two cappuccinos, but Peggy said she wanted hot cocoa. "Cocoa?" snapped the waitress. "We no hava no cocoa!"

I'll admit that for a moment I was embarrassed by my young date's lack of sophistication. But then the waitress caught Peggy's eyes and she paused. She must have seen something in those eyes, no doubt the same thing I saw, an innocence and purity that you just never expect to see in this modern world of ours. When she spoke again, her voice was soft.. "You no worry, *bambina*," she said as she patted Peggy's arm. "We maka you happy." As she trundled back to the kitchen she bellowed in a voice like a bullhorn, "Enrico! You maka this sweet littla girl some cocoa! *Capish'?*"

And in that moment I understood that there were more important things than sophistication.

"You have Splendid Powers I never knew about," I said.

She blushed and lowered her eyes. "Don't tease me. I'm nothing special. It's not like I'm an artist or a genius or…anything."

"Ah," I said, as the waitress brought our drinks and patted Peggy on the head. "You admire creativity. Has your cousin told you anything about me?"

She nodded her head eagerly and blurted out, "Oh, yes! He's told me all about…er…he did mention that you're a novelist."

"Well," I said, "I do like to write."

"Oh, I think literature is just marvy," she sighed, her eyes growing moony. "We're reading *A Separate Peace* in school."

"Ah. School," I said. "Just how old are you, Peggy?"

"I'm seventeen," she said. And quickly added, "But I'll be eighteen in March!"

I told myself I'd have to bridle the infatuation that was suddenly engulfing me. Even for a visitor from another planet, a statute is a statute. Besides, I wouldn't dream of offending the best pal a guy ever had.

Silence fell again. I could sense that she was trying to say something.

"Maybe…gulp…maybe you could write something for me sometime," she whispered.

"Only an ode could do you justice," I said. "But I'm afraid my powers of expression, even though they earned me a place among the ranks of the Array of Splendid Striplings, couldn't cut it when it came to putting your beauty into words." So much for bridling my infatuation.

"Oh, Will!" she breathed. "That was dreamy!"

I didn't know how to follow up on that. Which turned out to be fine because suddenly all we could hear was the squeal of tires. Four wise guys with machine guns burst into the cafe, aimed at the elderly man at the counter, and opened fire.

Suddenly Splendid Girl appeared before them, hands on hips, smiling confidently. The bullets bounced harmlessly off her indestructible, proud little breasts.

"Great Amundsen!" I thought to myself. "Peggy has betrayed her secret identity to the world!"

But when I turned in my seat, there sat Peggy Pearl Perkins, cup in hand.

"Wha…?" I said.

"I am a Peggy Pearl Perkins robot," she said. "My mistress summoned me with an ultrasonic command to preserve her secret identity."

Splendid Girl tucked the hitmen under her arm and said, "I'm taking you boys to jail where you can't do any more harm." With that, she vanished in a flash.

I found the robot to be charming company. It always amazes me, not only how lifelike the robots appear, but how Splendid Man and Splendid Girl have programmed them to have well-rounded personalities. I hope that someday I'll be able to create characters half as well for my fiction.

"I'll tell you a secret if you promise not to tell my mistress," said the robot.

"Cross my heart and hope to die," I said. For a moment I felt proud that I could speak in language that teenagers could relate to, until I realized that they probably hadn't talked like that since 1906.

"Splendid Girl has a crush on you," she giggled. "She uses the X-ray setting of her Splendid Vision to watch you all the time."

I felt myself blush and pulled my jacket closer around me. Then the robot, with that uncanny sensitivity of the young (or at least a precise simulation of it), said, "Oh, but don't worry. She always averts her vision when she's afraid she'll see something embarrassing."

"How long has this been going on?" I asked.

"Ever since you went on that mission with Splendid Man to the distant past and the sorceress Aeaea turned you into a horse."

"Yes, young girls do like horses," I mused.

"Her old boyfriend was the enchanted horse Cosmo, the Awesome Stud. But they broke up because he was just a dumb jock."

I remembered that Splendid Girl had had a lot of boyfriends. I didn't want to pry, but you know how obsessive a guy can get about these things. "She also used to go around with that fish boy, Finwad, didn't she?"

The robot made a face and said, "Ugh. She dropped him because he was conceited."

"What about the 30th Century Stripling Cerebriac 6.2, the one with the big brain?"

"Oh, he was a big bore." The robot took a sip of her cocoa. "She did like Apollo a whole lot, though."

"*Apollo*? The Greek and Roman god of manly beauty?"

"That's the one. But she decided she didn't like pretty boys. Then she went with Warren for a while, but he was too old for her."

"*That* Warren?"

The robot nodded. "I know what you're thinking. He's a pretty boy, too. It's a girl's prerogative to be inconsistent, you know! Let's see. Then there was Magic Johnson. Then Turgid Teen, the Splendid Hero from Andromeda. Then Keith Richards. Then..."

The robot must have noticed that I was turning colors, because she broke off quickly and added, "Of course, she never let any of them get past first base. When a Splendid Girl says no, she means no!"

"Thank God," I said, mopping the clammy sweat from my brow. "But if she's dated all these hotshots, why..."

"There's one kind of man she's never really known," whispered the robot, leaning confidentially toward me. "A writer."

"Never?" I asked, my hopes rising.

"Never," she said. "Well, she did get asked out once by J. D. Salinger, but he was too much of a sourpuss. Splendid Man says you're one of the few novelists who's also a really nice guy."

"Who else is going to show up on this list?" I asked. "Hugh Hefner? Ted Kennedy?"

She blushed. The blush didn't mean anything to me at first, until it occurred to me that robots don't blush. Then I realized that I was no longer talking to the robot. Apparently Splendid Girl had changed places with it at Splendid Speed.

"What was that mechanical minx telling you?" she demanded.

"Nothing," I said innocently.

"The rat!" said Peggy. "I'll rip out her circuitry! What's the world coming to when you can't trust your best robot?"

She grew sullen. To lighten her up I said, "I really admired the way you handled those killers. You saved the life of District Attorney Jenkins."

But Splendid Girl wasn't having any. It hadn't been so long since I'd been a teenager that I couldn't remember how prone they are to brooding.

There was nothing for it. I paid the check and got up to leave. But I wasn't going to let her mood defeat me. The robot had said Splendid Girl had a crush on me, and robots, at least those programmed with Splendid Man and Splendid Girl's moral code, never lie. It didn't matter if Peggy was in a snit or if she had dated a million guys. She had a crush on *me*, Will Jones, and I wasn't going to squander that!

But how? My mind raced furiously on the walk back to my apartment. I couldn't believe how this girl had burrowed her way into my heart in just one afternoon, like a Strontiumese Drill-Beast in an argon-bearing atmosphere, only different. I had to do just the right thing to salvage what I hoped was the beginning of a beautiful friendship. But what?

She wouldn't look at me when I held out my hand to say goodbye. Impulsively, I placed my index finger under her chin and tilted her head back.

"Kar'En," I said breathlessly, and kissed her softly on the lips. And with a surge of elation I realized that she had an "en" in her name!

She trembled and closed her eyes. I said, "Can I see you again?"

"Of course you can," she whispered. "If you…gulp…want to."

"Then can I call you?"

"Why waste all that money on long-distance calls? Here." She put a heart-shaped hairbrush into my hand. "Signal me with this whenever you want to. Just vibrate the bristles. I'll be able to hear it from anywhere within two hundred light years. I'll call it our Date Brush. But remember, I go to school Monday through Friday until three o'clock."

I stuck the brush in my jacket pocket. "Thank you, Kar'En," I said.

"You're welcome, Will," she said.

"I like you very much, Kar'En," I said.

"Me too, Will," she said.

"Sigh," I said.

"Sigh," she said.

"I'd like to walk you home," I said, but even as I said it I realized that to walk this girl home I'd have to learn to fly at Splendid Speed.

"I'm sorry, I have to hurry," she said. "My foster father wants me in by dark, since it's a school night." She changed instantaneously to her Splendid Girl garb, so fast that I was unable to gallantly turn my back.

She streaked into the sky, but before she vanished from sight she blew me a kiss with her Splendid Breath. In her excitement, the little dear blew a bit too hard, knocking me senseless against the gate of my apartment building.

Episode Twelve
When Will Regained His Self-Esteem

"Oh, Will," she said. "Isn't life wonderful?"

"Wonderful," I said.

She hugged me and her body felt good. And warm. Especially warm. It was damn cold atop Mount Everest, lovely view or no. But Splendid Girl, with the romanticism of the young, would accept no substitute in her quest for a secluded rendezvous.

"Oh, Will," she sighed, resting her golden-tressed head on my shoulder and gazing at the Himalayan scenery. "Oh, thank you for rustling your Date Brush and summoning me ultrasonically. After every date I'm afraid you'll decide you'd rather have on older, more sophisticated girlfriend who can talk to you about literature and life and Pernod and things. Like that Didion person. Or Sylvia Plath."

"But Sylvia Plath's been dead for years!"

"See? If she was still alive you'd probably rather be with..."

"Stop being ridiculous," I said. "How do you think I feel? I'm always afraid you'll get bored with a bookworm like me, and a non-Splendid Powered bookworm to boot. Especially when I think of those Splendid Jerks you used to go around with, like Finwad, the fish boy, and that enchanted horse, Cosmo the Awesome Stud."

"Oh Will, my Will, don't be silly!" she cried. "Do you think I could ever have come here to share this scenery with Finny, or gone to a jazz concert with Studly? You're the only man for me, Will."

"Really?"

"Really!"

"You *really* like me better than Burt Reynolds?"

"Don't be silly. All he ever did was brag about the time he

posed naked in *Cosmopolitan.*"

"Or Dirkie, the Crimson Spear's teen sidekick?"

"Gag me with a spoon!"

"Even better than Rick James?"

"Ugh. He was way too freaky for me!"

"Kiss me, baby."

"But Will," she said, blushing and glancing around. "What if someone's watching?"

"No one can see us here, Kar'En," I said, "unless your cousin Splendid Man is training the telescopic setting of his Splendid Vision on us. But he told me he would be busy on a mission in outer space with the North American Alliance for Meetness all weekend."

"Jeepers, isn't that a silly name, Will?" said Kar'En. "I wish my cousin had known you before they came up with it. I bet you, with your power of Splendid Wording, could've come up with something way better."

"I would have liked something with the word 'league' in it," I mused. "But enough of this nonsense."

I caught her up in my arms and kissed her. Her firm young figure melted against me. I almost laid her down on the perennial ice cap and made her mine right there and then, no matter what the laws of Strontium or California might say. Besides, who knows what the moral statutes of far-off Nepal are like? But when I remembered her Splendid Powers I turned to jelly. How could I satisfy her in life and love? After all, would you be satisfied with a lover who could boast only a knowledge of books, a wry sense of humor, and a gift for lucid narrative, if you were endowed with Splendid Strength, Splendid Speed, Vacuum Breath, and a trim, perfect little body?

"What's wrong, my darling?" she asked softly. With her extraordinary sensitivity, she had immediately detected my insecurity. Maybe it was the way my knees were shaking.

"These…these past few weeks have been so wonderful," I stammered, "but I can't shake the fear that they just can't last. I keep thinking that any minute you'll come to your senses and see that I'm just a nobody. Sometimes I'm convinced that the only way you could love me is if you'd been exposed to lavender strontiumite."

She put her hands on her hips and frowned. "Will, when did we first kiss?"

"Seventeen days ago."

"When did I first tell you I love you?"

"Six days ago."

"And how long does it take the unpredictable effects of lavender strontiumite to wear off?"

"Forty-eight hours," I said sheepishly.

"Now who's being ridiculous?" she said. Then she threw her arms around me. "Oh, Will, my silly Will! How can I prove to you how much you mean to me?" She gazed at me with those big limpid eyes of hers and sighed. "Not all the Splendid Powers of every Strontiumese native who ever miraculously survived the Great Flood of Strontium and ended up on Earth, with its argon-tinged atmosphere and lesser gravity, could give me what you've given me, my love."

She pressed her yearning little mouth against mine. I began breathing heavily, but then I felt dizzy. Maybe it's not such a swift idea to get worked up at 29,028 feet above sea level.

"Oh, poor Will," she said. "Here, let me wrap you in my indestructible cape and fly you down to a nicer altitude before you faint. I'll tell you what, why don't we visit some of our favorite romantic places? Since it's Saturday, I don't have to be home until 11:00 P.M. Eastern Daylight Time."

Her words had quieted my fears for the moment. But as we zoomed across the Himalayas and into India I felt my self-confidence crumbling. Bundled up in her indestructible cape like a babe in swaddling clothes, I was more conscious than ever of my inadequacy. Sure, I quoted Kipling as we strolled through the colorful bazaars of Bombay. Sure, I discoursed on the development of the French Rococo under the decadence of the Bourbon Dynasty when we popped into the Louvre, until Kar'En's eyes shone in admiration like moons. But think how I felt when she used her

Splendid Vision to first boil and sterilize, then cool, the water offered us by kindly Algerian beggars in the labyrinthine backstreets of the Casbah. Think how useless I felt when, upon our arrival in Rio, she used her Splendid Breath to turn away a tropical storm that would have spoiled our evening walk on the beach. This little girl would never need me to open pickle jars, bring in bags of groceries from the car, or kill spiders in the bathtub. How long could a girl accustomed to dating Splendid Heroes keep loving the least heroic man on Earth?

Suddenly, as we strolled on the sand, Splendid Girl fell against me.

"Oh Will...gasp...suddenly...gasp...so weak," she gasped.

I caught her in my arms. All her Splendid Strength fled her. Her face paled, then took on a silvery tint. "Kar'En!" I cried. "What's happened? Is it strontiumite?"

"L-look!" she gasped. "A Strontiumese Space Cat, whose silver strontiumite fur renders me weak and helpless! It must have miraculously escaped Strontium's doom! Save me from it, Will!"

Indeed, where she pointed with her trembling hand, I saw a glowing silver feline flying circles in the air. Then, as Kar'En collapsed to her knees, it flew at her, hissing and spitting, as if to rake her to death with its adamantine claws. Instinctively, I jumped between the creature and its prey. As it circled over us, preparing to pounce, I adopted what I hoped was a combat stance. Then it swooped in. After that I wasn't aware of much of anything except flashing teeth, fishy breath, the feel of fur and sinew in my hands, and a feral yowling that could have come either from the cat or from me. The next thing I knew, I was hurling the thing into the air. Then I saw the Space Cat vanishing into the coffee-black Brazilian sky, its vivid stars like sugar lumps.

I turned to the prostrate Splendid Girl. To my horror, I discovered that a fine strontiumite dust had settled over her.

"Groan," she said.

"Courage, Kar'En," I said. I drew her lithe form to me and rushed her down the golden beach to the sea. I let the gentle, tropic waters of the South Atlantic wash away her pain. I kissed her there in the waves and her eyes fluttered open.

"Oh, Will," she said. "This is just like *From Here to Eternity*."

"Very good, baby," I said with a grin. "Remember the director?"

She cast her gaze about as if searching for something, then turned her big orbs on me as they gleamed with tears of joy and love. "Fred Zinnemann!" she squealed, and threw her arms around me. "Oh, Will, you've taught me so much!" She sighed and snuggled into my grasp. "I wish I could stay like this forever, but my foster father said I can't stay out late with a boy he's never met. Oh, Will, come with me to Axial Town, my foster city! I want you to meet my foster parents!"

I don't mind saying it. For once, I felt like a man, even wrapped head to toe in Kar'En's indestructible cape.

We landed at the edge of a sleepy town not far from Municipalitus. Kar'En changed into her pigtailed Peggy Pearl Perkins identity in a blur of motion. I'd gotten used to her changing so fast that I never got to see anything, but I still couldn't help feeling a tad disappointed. Hand in hand we walked along the peaceful streets until we came to one bright little cottage.

Maybe you're like me, and you always get cold feet when you're put on display. After all, what could I show for myself in the way of future prospects and security when Peggy presented me to her foster parents? On any previous night I would have backed out. But tonight, with the memory of the retreating Space Cat still in my mind, I knew I could handle anything. As Kar'En let me in and I came face to face with kindly Mr. Perkins, Axial Town's leading engineer, and his kindly wife, Mrs. Perkins, I was determined to prove to them that I was the man for their little girl.

"Well, well, well, this must be Will," said Mr. Perkins, shaking my hand. "I'm relieved to see that Peggy's beau from San Francisco hasn't shown up in tie-dye and love beads!"

"Oh, daddy," Peggy said cutely.

"Have a seat on the davenport, son," said Mr. Perkins. "Put your feet up on the ottoman. Bring this fine young fellow a cup of hot cocoa, dear."

Mrs. Perkins smiled and bustled off. Mr. Perkins gave me a friendly but appraising glance, taking note of my polyester slacks, black turtleneck, and gray tweed.

"Tell me, Will, what do you do?" he asked.

"I'm...er...temporarily between jobs," I said. "I was in beds for a while."

"Oh dear! Were you ill?" called Mrs. Perkins from the kitchen.

"No, ma'am, I mean I was a bed salesman," I explained. "But I'm planning on going into books."

"Selling them?" asked Mr. Perkins.

"No...er...writing them," I said.

"Oh daddy, Will's a wonderful writer!" interjected Peggy.

"Well," I said hesitantly, "I do like to..."

"Have you ever considered finding yourself a good bookstore and working there?" asked Mr. Perkins. "Or hooking up with the Britannica people? Nothing beats a steady door-to-door sales job."

I decided to take the initiative. "Mr. Perkins, let me assure you that if your foster daughter's welfare ever comes to depend on me, I will do everything in my power to make her as comfortable and secure as she deserves."

Mr. Perkins nodded thoughtfully. Then he said, "Will, I know a fellow of your age and facial hair must have had some experience with women. Is there anything you'd like to...er..."

"Well, to tell you the truth, sir," I volunteered, "I was engaged once. My fiancée ended it, but she made it clear that it had nothing to do with my prospects. She just felt she had to leave me to find herself."

"She was one of those modern girls, Daddy," said Peggy with evident distaste.

"Tsk tsk tsk," said Mrs. Perkins, bringing the cocoa.

"I'm afraid she felt a little inferior to me," I said.

"Our Peggy won't!" said Mrs. Perkins, winking at her husband. "She's a splendid girl!"

"Sh! Irma! Careful!" hissed Mr. Perkins. "You might accidentally reveal Peggy's secret you-know-what!"

"Oh, don't worry, Mr. Perkins, Mrs. Perkins," I said quickly. "I already know that your foster daughter is secretly Splendid Girl, the Princess of Potency!"

"Omigosh!" gasped Mr. Perkins.

"How…ulp…do you know that?" asked Mrs. Perkins.

"Will is Splendid Man's best pal!" chirped Peggy.

"Well, second to his old pal Bobby Anderssen, that albino cub reporter, of course," I said.

"Son, why didn't you tell us this before?" beamed Mr. Perkins, clapping me on the shoulder. "Any pal of Splendid Man's is a pal of mine! And any intentions you have for my little foster girl are fine by me! I'm sure they'll be honorable."

Suddenly I was a member of the family. A smile split my face from ear to ear and was mirrored on the faces of the Perkinses. Even the family cat, a fluffy calico, appeared from under a couch to rub itself against my legs.

For some reason, that seemed to upset Peggy. "Awp! Blotchy!" she cried. " What are you doing here?"

But before I could puzzle over her reaction, Mr. Perkins drew me aside and said to me privately, "As you know, Will, I hold a respected position in this community with Axial Town Engineering."

"Yes sir, Mr. Perkins," I said.

"Call me Ted, Will," he said. "I'll tell you what, son. Come to work for me, and I can guarantee you a good salary with plenty of room for advancement. You strike me as a real go-getter, Willy-boy, just the kind of fellow I want in my organization and in my family. Axial Town's a friendly place, and you could take night classes over at Stantheman College to keep up with your cultural things, if you must. I'll tell you one thing, Will. This is a great community in which to raise a family. You think about it."

I was touched beyond words. I could only look at my feet in embarrassment. It was then that I noticed the silver dust on my pant-leg, where the cat had been rubbing.

I looked for the animal. Peggy had him in her arms and was scolding him.

"Naughty Blotchy!" she was saying. "I told you to fly up into outer space and play with Stronto the Splendid Dog at his Doghouse of Contemplation until Will was gone!"

"Don't scold your poor Splendid Cat, Peggy," I said. "It's better that I know the truth. Did you command Blotchy ultrasonically to color himself with silver dust and pretend to be a Strontiumese Space Cat while you feigned weakness?"

"But...but Will," she stammered. "I only wanted to make you stop worrying that you weren't good enough for me. I never want anything to come between us, Will. Oh, but now you must hate me!" Tears brimmed in her big gentle eyes and spilled onto her cheeks. She lowered her head and ran from the room. I caught her arm to stop her. With her Splendid Strength, she had dragged me some yards before she noticed me and stopped.

I rose to my feet. I placed my forefinger beneath her chin and tipped her head back. I murmured, "You went through all that...just for me? Oh, you little fool, how can I hate you?" I kissed away the salty tears from one cheek, and then from the other. Then I kissed her trembling lips.

"Will," she said.

"Kar'En," I said.

"Sigh," she said.

"Ditto," I said.

"Oh Ted, just look at them!" sighed Mrs. Perkins. "Isn't young love wonderful?"

Episode Thirteen
Splendid Man's Most Embarassing Evening

Splendid Man once mentioned to me that his favorite dish when he was a tot on Strontium, the planet of his birth on which all life had been destroyed by a great flood, had been crystal-snake stew. Even though I may not have the power of Splendid Recall, I always make it a point to remember things like that. You never know when they'll come in handy.

Like tonight, for instance. Tonight was a very special occasion, and only the best cuisine could grace our table. I had gotten the recipe for the stew from Splendid Girl, and spent the entire day in the kitchen preparing my pal's favorite dish.

Naturally, I didn't have a crystal snake to work with. Even had one of those reptiles miraculously escaped Strontium's doom, it would have been invulnerable under Earth's argon-tinged atmosphere and lesser gravity, and therefore impossible to cook. But like all good chefs, you learn to make substitutions when the exact ingredients are unavailable. In this case, I remembered Splendid Man saying that crystal snake tasted like chicken, so I picked up the plumpest fryer I could find.

I was standing over the stove stirring the stew when my dining room window suddenly exploded.

"Oh, no," I called from the kitchen. "Is it seven already?"

"Seven on the nose, Will," Splendid Man said.

"Sorry," I said. "I forgot to leave the window open."

"I'm the one who should be sorry, Will," Splendid Man said. "I shouldn't have been flying so fast that I wasn't able to slacken my speed when I saw that the window was closed. It wouldn't have happened if I hadn't been installing some wainscoting in my lunar Citadel of Contemplation, lost track of the time myself, and left with only half a nanosecond to spare."

"I won't let you take the blame, pal," I insisted.

"Well, I'll tell you what, pal," he said. "After dinner, I'll fly down to the beach and fashion a new window from the sand."

"That would be swell," I said.

Suddenly, Splendid Man drew up short. "That smell!" he exclaimed. "That can only be Strontiumese crystal-snake stew!"

"Your sense of Splendid Smell never fails you, does it?" I asked.

"But, Will," he cried, "where the heck did you get ahold of a crystal snake?"

"Er...that's for me to know and you to find out," I said, deciding he would be happier if I let him believe we were having the real article. And keeping him happy tonight was a priority.

"It smells fantastic, Will."

"Thanks, Cal," I said, beaming with pride.

Even though Splendid Man can live interminably without food and drink, he ate voraciously of the stew and drank glass after glass of the cabernet that had cost me half a paycheck from my temporary job as roast carver at a buffet. I didn't have a chance to break the news to him until we were sipping our café royales.

"Cal, I said. "I...er...have something to tell you."

"Why, Will," Splendid Man said. "I haven't seen you so nervous since you accompanied me on a mission in space and helped me repel an invasion of Altairian Mud Fiends. What is it?"

"Well, I need to ask your permission for something," I stammered.

"What, Will? Go on."

"Well, haven't you wondered why I haven't complained about being lonely of late?"

"Actually, Will," he said, "I've wondered why I've seen so little of you of late."

With a pang, I suddenly realized that I'd been neglecting my big buddy. I started to apologize, then decided to forge on with my announcement. It would explain, if not excuse, my neglect.

"Well, you see, pal," I gulped, "I'm engaged to be married."

Cal gazed at me with a look of utter stupefaction. Then, seeming to recover himself, he said, "But that's wonderful news, pal. Who's the lucky girl?"

"Well…er…you see…"

"And why the heck would you need *my* permission?"

I took a deep breath and poured it out. "Because my fiancée is none other than your Splendid Cousin, Kar'En!"

I know this is hard to believe, but Splendid Man's skin actually turned white. Fleetingly, I wondered if maybe some silver strontiumite flakes had gotten mixed in with the poppy seed (an excellent substitute for Strontiumese gloppo seed, by the way) I'd put in the stew.

"Speak to me, pal," I choked.

Then that Splendid Epidermis changed color again, this time to a red so livid that it rivaled the costume of the Crimson Spear. I was reminded of the incident retold in the comics as "The Bizarre Transformations of the Chameleon Splendid Man." But not even the most lurid effects ever achieved by four-color ink dots could approximate the chromatic oscillations transpiring before my eyes. Splendid Man pushed his chair back so hard that the legs dug furrows in my no-wax floor. He jumped to his feet and started pacing furiously about my dining room.

I don't mind admitting this, but he terrified me at that moment. For once, I was able to fully appreciate the intrepidity that such evil villains as Steamy, the Water Vapor Creature, Sir Qwertyuiop, that wicked fairy from the 37th Dimension, and Plasto, the Man with the Strontiumite Spleen, display again and again when pitting themselves against an angry Man of Splendor.

At length, he stopped pacing, turned a baleful glance upon me, and roared, "I can't believe that you, my best pal next to Bobby Anderssen, that albino cub reporter, could do such a thing!"

"Do what, Cal?" I gasped, desperately clutching the edge of the table to anchor myself against the sonic onslaught he was suddenly hurling at me.

"How could you possibly even consider wedding a girl who is still a *minor*?!" he bellowed.

It was no use. I lost my grip and fell over backwards, chair and all.

"She hasn't even graduated from high school!" he boomed. "She still wears her hair in pigtails when in her Peggy Pearl Perkins secret identity! For Amundsen's sake, Will, she still dreams about *horses!*"

I didn't move. Sprawled out on the floor, the sonic waves passed harmlessly over me.

"And besides, when she *is* finally ready to wed, it should be to someone Splendid like herself! Someone like Finwad, the fish boy from Lemuria, or Cerebriac 6.2, the Stripling with the Positronic Brain from the 8th Dimension!"

That got my goat. Like a sailor struggling to keep at the helm in a typhoon, I grimly righted myself. "Listen, pal," I shouted, "and listen good. You're not talking to any Joe Blow on the street. You happen to be talking to Literary Lad, honorary member of the Array of Splendid Striplings, that glittering band of teenagers in the 30th Century. Furthermore, you happen to be addressing the mascot of the North American Alliance for Meetness, that gathering of the world's greatest Splendid Stars. What gives you the right, just because you're the greatest hero of them all, to decide I'm not Splendid enough for your cousin?"

My words were like a shower of silver strontiumite meteors, suddenly dampening his fury.

"I'm sorry, Will," he said, slumping in a chair. "I didn't mean to suggest that at all. I'm as quick as anyone to admire your phenomenal dexterity with words. I admit I was wrong to imply that Finwad, Cerebriac 6.2, or even Cosmo, the Awesome Stud, could make a better husband for her. But still, Will. She's so young. So very young."

"Maybe she's physically young," I retorted, still a little hot under the collar, "but she's certainly not emotionally immature. As Doc Quackeray, that brilliant scientist, recently noted in an important paper, girls endowed with Splendid Powers mature much faster than their peers. I think you know as well as I do that Splendid Girl is every inch a woman. Besides, I've vowed not to marry her until she turns eighteen."

"You're right," Cal said, hanging his head. "You're absolutely right. She is very mature for her years. Like the time she chose to sacrifice her own life in order to rescue her foster parents, Ted and Irma Perkins, from the machinations of that master criminal of the Ghost World, Casp'Er, entirely unaware that Blotchy the Splendid Cat had already cleverly summoned a pair of Ted and Irma robots to deceive Casp'Er and make her demise unnecessary. Or the time…"

"Or the time she gave her heart to the man who loves her and will care for her for the rest of her days," I said calmly.

He looked at me then with eyes filled with tears, and spoke in a voice so fraught with emotion that I could never effectively convey it on the page unless I were to punctuate his sentence with words like "choke" and "gulp."

"I'm sure you do love her, Will. It's just that…I love her too. And I'd imagined…a different future for her, that's all."

That's when it hit me. "Oh, geez, Cal," I said. "Of course. How could I be so blind?"

He looked searchingly at me. "Blind…?"

"I understand, Cal. I understand at last why you've never proposed marriage to Pepper Pine, and why your romance with your old mermaid sweetheart Pura Poseidonis of Lemuria mysteriously broke down into a bittersweet friendship, and why, with Patti Pert and countless millions of other beautiful women throwing themselves at you, you've always held yourself aloof! Cal, I understand!"

"You…you do?"

"Yes, Cal! You've been saving yourself for your cousin Splendid Girl!"

He frowned. "What?"

"I'm sorry, Cal," I said, putting my hand on his arm. "It must be so lonely, being the most Splendid of all Splendid Heroes. Of course you yearn for a soulmate of splendor equal to your own. And here you are, putting your loneliness aside to help me meet girls and build up my confidence, and what happens but…"

"No. Will. Whoa. Stop."

"You don't have to hide it from me, pal. I…"

"Will. Listen to me. Kar'En is a Splendid Girl indeed, whether you capitalize the words or not. But even though first cousins are allowed to marry in most countries on Earth and several American states, Kar'En and I are from Strontium, where it's unlawful."

"The heart knows no laws, as a wise man once…"

"Will? Pal? Will you just take my word for it that I don't have, and never have had, any romantic interest in my cousin? My feelings for her are entirely…not parental, exactly, but…"

"Avuncular?"

"Yes, Will. Your prodigious vocabulary has come through again. My feelings for Kar'En are entirely avuncular. All I care about is her happiness."

"Does this mean you're giving us your blessing, pal?"

"Promise me she'll finish college, Will."

"You know how I value education, pal. So does this mean you're giving us your blessing?"

"And hold off on having children, Will. She needs to grow up more herself before she takes on that responsibility."

"As do I, pal, as do I. So are you giving us your blessing *now*?"

"And please be careful. As you know, I've always feared that my enemies would try to strike at me through my loved ones. As Splendid Girl's husband, you'll be very vulnerable to the attacks of her many foes."

I have to admit that gave me pause. Splendid Girl has some formidable enemies—like Pandoro, the evil warlock, and Clammy, the Slime Mold from Ganymede—who could do away with me in two shakes of the leg, and I'm not exactly a paragon of manly courage. But nothing was going to stop me from gaining his consent when I was so close. "Cal, you and I have been pals for months now," I said, "and has Giganto the Splendid Mandrill tried to peel me like a banana, or has the Vengeance Is Mine Squad threatened to turn me into a waffle if you didn't surrender yourself into their clutches?"

"No, but…

"Please tell me I have your blessing now."

He hesitated. "There's just one more thing," he finally said, "and it's not meant to be a condition. Only a request. A small request."

"Anything," I said.

He gave me a smile, but it looked forced. "Just don't forget your old pal," he said. "Okay?"

Even though he tried to toss it off lightly, I could tell it was anything but. "Not a chance," I said, touched beyond words. "Not in a million years!"

"Glad to hear it, pal!" he said, and this time the smile he flashed me was genuine. He stood up and clapped a hand on my shoulder. "You have my blessings, pal. If Kar'En truly feels ready to get married, then I'm glad it will be to a true pal like you. I've got to level with you, I was getting pretty worried when she was dating Turgid Boy, the Hero from Andromeda."

"That's swell of you, pal," I said. We just stood there for a few seconds, him smiling at me expectantly. "That's truly swell," I added.

He must have caught on that something was still bothering me, because his look of expectancy turned to one of puzzlement and he asked, "Is there something else you wanted to tell me, Will?"

"Actually, Cal...the truth is..." I fumbled, "there is...actually...well...something I kind of want to ask you."

After another long silence he said, "But you're not sure how to ask me, is that it?"

I nodded, probably several more times than I had to.

"You know you can ask me anything, don't you, pal?"

I took a deep breath, and then I plunged in. "Sure, Cal," I said shakily. "It's just that...I've gathered that Kar'En isn't very...experienced."

He frowned thoughtfully. "Well, it's true that she hasn't put in nearly as many years as a defender of Earth as I have," he said, "nor as most of my pals in the North American Alliance for..."

"No, Cal," I said hastily. "I mean...more *personal* experience."

He looked confused.

"More *intimate* experience."

He still looked confused. I finally had to accept the fact that euphemisms just weren't going to cut it. "What I'm saying, Cal," I said, "is that I'm fairly sure Kar'En is a…virgin."

It was as if a dark cloud crossed his face. "You're…*fairly* sure?" Then the words exploded from his throat at such Splendid Amplitude that they blew out all my remaining windows. "Of course she's a virgin! Have you forgotten that she was raised in a Strontiumese generation starship on which all life, except hers, was lost when the air and provisions ran out? Do you think she's some Earthling tart? Of *course* she's a virgin! Why, on the old planet, no self-respecting girl would even *think* of giving herself to a man before her wedding night!"

For the first time I detected a trace of a Strontiumese accent in Cal's speech.

I asked, "Were all natives of Strontium really that morally upright?"

The anger left his voice as he answered, "Well, not really. But in addition to Splendid Strength and Splendid Speed, we've developed the power of Splendid Virtue under Earth's argon-tinged atmosphere and lesser gravity."

"Of course," I said, grateful for the change of topic. "That explains your unfailing selflessness and good judgment in all your work as Earth's self-appointed benefactor, except when exposed to bizarre and malignant influences such as lavender strontiumite, or evil magic such as practiced by the ancient sorceress Aeaea who, incidentally, once turned me into a horse."

He nodded thoughtfully. "Like the time lavender strontiumite caused my eyebrows to fall off and I became as twisted and evil as my archnemesis, Pox Pascal."

"I remember," I said. "Those were tense times."

He sat down and gave me a weary smile. "Well, now that we've covered that…"

"Actually…."

He lost his smile. "What more, Will?"

"Well, you see…I brought up your cousin's…inexperience for

a very specific reason."

"Yes?"

"The thing is...if the bodies of all Strontiumese are entirely invulnerable...or shall we say *impenetrable*...well..."

I waited for him to catch on. He didn't.

"That is to say," I continued, "if no part of Kar'En's body...not even a single *membrane*...can be *broken*, then..."

"Yes, Will?"

"Don't you understand, Cal? If every part of her girlish body is not only invulnerable but *intact*...then, well, things might be a little...er....difficult the first time we...er..."

He stared at me uncomprehendingly for a while. His eyebrows shot up when he got it. "Oh, my. That is a problem."

He began pacing the room nervously. He furrowed his brow in thought. "Let's see," he said. "I can whisk you off to my Citadel of Contemplation on the moon, where I can use one of my Splendid Devices to grant you temporary Splendid Powers great enough to...er..."

"That'll work!" I said.

"The trouble with that is that I've granted Splendid Powers to others, like my pal Bobby, in the past, and every time they've affected the personality of the recipient. Even the nicest folks become dangerous menaces when they suddenly find themselves Splendid. It takes time to learn that with Splendid Power there must also come Splendid Responsibility."

"But, pal. I only want Splendid Powers long enough to...er..."

"I know, pal. But I'd hate to see my little cousin's wedding night spoiled by a groom gone rogue."

"What if Kar'En and I honeymoon on a planet with an argon-free atmosphere?" I suggested. "Since natives of Strontium lose their Splendid Powers on an argon-less planet, she'd be no more Splendid than me and I'd easily be able to...er..."

"Ingenious, Will!" exclaimed Splendid Man. "In fact, that might be a good way to start up the marriage, with the two of you on equal terms. Then, when you come back to Earth's argon-tinged atmosphere, her invulnerability will no longer pose a problem, as her...er... that is to say, you'll have already...er...there'll no longer be...er..."

"Got it," I said.

He exhaled in evident relief and made as if to dry off his brow, even though his Splendid Pores don't sweat and his brow was perfectly dry. "Well, then, Will, I imagine that wraps up all your concerns. There's nothing left for me to say but congratulations. Right, Will? That's all that's left for me to say?"

"Well, actually..." I began.

Then I stopped. There was one more thing bothering me: Namely, whether the unyielding quality of Kar'En's breasts when I embraced her was due to her own Strontiumese invulnerability or, as I hoped, to the affect of Earth's argon-tinged atmosphere and lesser gravity on her undergarments. But as he waited for me to continue, Cal looked as miserable as when Pox Pascal had tossed that lump of strontiumite at his feet in ancient Alexandria.

"I do have one more question," I said.

"All right, Will," he said glumly.

I asked, "Do you really, truly give us your blessing, pal?"

I'd never seen him look more relieved. "I do, pal," he said. "I really, truly do!" Then my future cousin-in-law smiled and shook my hand.

Episode Fourteen
The Green-Eyed Monster from Earth

And there she was, kissing the fish boy Finwad smack on the lips and thinking, "Yummy! This dreamboat can really kiss!"

I'd been wrestling with myself for weeks, but finally I hadn't been able to suppress my morbid curiosity any longer, and I'd broken out my collection of *Commotion Comics, Featuring Splendid Girl*. After leafing through a couple I'd come across the Finwad scene above, and now I discovered that in the very next issue she was smooching with Cerebriac 6.2, he of the Positronic Brain from the 8th Dimension.

"Jeepers!" she was thinking, as she clinched with the blue-skinned Stripling. "Who would have ever thought an egghead could kiss like this?!"

With trembling hands I checked out the next few issues. They were mostly innocuous adventures—Splendid Girl has to grapple with one of her robots who has gone rogue; an evil Strontorian invents an Exchange Ray that enables her to trade places with Kar'En; the Cuckoo Splendid Girl, one of those imperfect duplicates of Splendid Man and all his friends, comes to Earth looking for her twisted version of romance—but in the next issue she was at it again, this time with the enchanted horse Cosmo, the Awesome Stud. The story took place during a full moon, which enabled Cosmo to take on his human identity of Hoss Tamer, rancher and horse breeder extraordinaire, and there they were by the moonlit corral, osculating like fiends, and Kar'En thinking, "Golly! Golly! Golly!"

I threw the comic against the wall.

It was my day off from my temporary job at the messenger service, so I had plenty of time to sit around wallowing in my own obsessive thoughts. And it didn't take long for all the fears I'd been stifling for weeks to come bubbling up. Did Splendid Girl really want to marry me, Will Jones? How was that possible? Wasn't that simply too good to be true? I'd read enough comics to know that in the world of Splendid Heroes things are not often what they seem. I'd shaken the idea that she might have been exposed to lavender strontiumite, but now I found myself wondering if there might not be some other explanation for why she seemed to love me. Might she have to pretend to be engaged to me as part of an elaborate ruse to trap her archfoe Cerebria? Could she have regretted turning down J. D. Salinger and decided to date me to make him jealous?

At that point I knew I was just making myself crazy. I had to stop thinking, so I turned to the best antidote to thought I knew of, my television. I flicked it on—and my eyes were assaulted by a scene of utter mayhem!

Two cars were having a fistfight. No, not the drivers. The vehicles had grown arms and were pounding on each other like Larry Holmes and Randall "Tex" Cobb. If Larry Holmes were an old Plymouth Barracuda and Tex Cobb were a Dodge Charger, that is. A lamppost that had apparently developed the power to slither like a snake had snatched up some fat kid in its coils. A toaster on little legs was shooting Pop Tarts at passersby. The voice of a hysterical newscaster was reporting that all machines in the city of Municipalitus had suddenly come to life and were attacking each other and the populace at large.

The picture changed to a helicopter feed in which, hovering above the city, a little man seemed to float in mid-air, and I realized with a pang of dismay that it was Sir Qwertyuiop, that wicked fairy from the 37th Dimension who is always plaguing Splendid Man with his fiendish pranks. The newsman explained that this was but the latest in a rash of recent attacks by the malefic pixie, who had recently been specifically targeting Splendid Man's friends, like Pepper Pine, Bobby Anderssen, and Oliver Hazard Black, and now had apparently decided to visit his fiendishness upon the entirety of our hero's adopted city.

And suddenly everything made sense. The most horrible imaginable sense.

Then Splendid Man zoomed into the TV picture. He came to a stop before Sir Qwertyuiop, and they proceeded to argue vociferously, with many an angry hand gesture for emphasis. Sir Qwertyuiop waggled his top-hatted head, peered dramatically over the tops of his giant Elton John glasses, and whirled about to flounce the tail of his sequined velvet dinner coat in Splendid Man's direction. Suddenly, the iniquitous imp vanished in a puff of a smoke, and for a moment I wondered if Splendid Man had tricked him yet again into reciting all the letters on the top row of a typewriter keyboard from right to left, the only way to banish him back to the dimension of his origin for seventy-two weeks, fourteen hours, and thirty-eight minutes.

But as the cameras switched back to the city streets, all I could think of were the newscaster's words.

I whipped out my SOS Comb and vibrated the teeth. Splendid Man appeared so swiftly that for an instant I could have sworn I could see him on the television screen and hovering outside my window simultaneously. I opened the window and he wafted in.

"Hi, pal," he said.

"Hi, pal," I said. "I just saw you banish that fairy back to his own dimension on TV."

"I wish that were so," he said, peering at the TV screen. The picture now showed that all had been restored to normal. "I just persuaded him to put everything right, and he vanished on his own. I don't know what he's fiendishly planning this time."

"They said on the news that he's been targeting your friends lately. They mentioned Pepper and Bobby and Oliver Hazard. Do you know if he's gone after anybody else?"

"I know he was pestering Patti Pert, my boyhood friend from Turnipville, just last week. Why do you ask?"

"Do you think he'll come after me?"

"Anything's possible, Will. Be vigilant, and take nothing for granted."

I nodded. Hoarsely, I said, "Maybe you should go check on

some of your other pals now to make sure they're okay."

"Very thoughtful of you, Will," he said.

The moment he zoomed off I threw myself on my couch in utter despair. Take nothing for granted, he'd said! Indeed, I had taken far too much for granted, but now it all came clear. I'd always known how ridiculous, how pathetic it was to imagine that Splendid Girl, the Doll of Dynamism, the Servitress of Stupendousness, the idol of billions, the ex-girlfriend of every hotshot in the universe, could ever love an insignificant mug like me. But the part I hadn't understood was why she pretended to do so.

The answer was so simple. Splendid Girl had never pretended to love me at all. She had never kissed me, never whispered sweet nothings in my ear, never blushingly consented to be my bride. It had been Sir Qwertyuiop impersonating her all along!

As awful as the realization made me feel, it brought some relief as well. It's a horrible thing to fool yourself, and something of a consolation to finally wake up, even from the sweetest dream imaginable. Far better to face reality squarely, to admit that Splendid Girl could never marry the likes of me, than to go on deluding myself. Or, more to the point, letting that horrible sprite delude me!

The deception had to stop. As of now.

We'd made a date for that night to eat *asado* in Buenos Aires, but when she—I mean, *he*—arrived, I feigned a headache and insisted that I'd prefer to stay in.

"Oh, Will," he cried, "I hate to see you in pain! Let's go scour the earth for some silver strontiumite so I can share in your discomfort."

"That's okay," I said.

"Kiss me, darling."

It was all I could do not to throw up thinking of the pinched little imp lips I was kissing, even if they looked and felt like succulent strawberries.

"You lie down now, darling," he said, "and let sweetums bring you a cold compress."

I knew what I had to do, but suddenly I didn't want to do it. I guess I wanted to pretend a little longer that he truly was a lovely goddess who adored me. I threw myself on my bed and let him lay the compress on my head. He sat beside me on the bed, his beautiful bare legs stretched straight out, the dainty feet tucked into those darling red boots. I gazed at his small but perky breasts, and realized that I would never know if they were soft and yielding. I gazed at the hem of his skirt, dreaming of the glory beneath it—but then recoiling when I remembered what really lurked there.

I nudged him aside and stood up.

"I have a story that needs typing, darling," I said. "Would you mind terribly doing it for me if I read it aloud it to you?"

"Of course not, dear," he said, with a voice that sounded like the song of meadowlarks to my ears but that I knew was really a sibilant, nasal whine. "I've been learning to type in school and I'm up to 3,678,393,215 words a minute."

I really did have a story I was working on, but I'd made some special revisions to it just prior to his arrival. He typed as I read from my handwritten draft. I could have sprung my trick on him at any time, but still I could not bring myself to drag my illusion to its final and irrevocable end, so I read the bulk of it to him. At last, it could be put off no longer.

"My eyes hurt, muffin," I said, "and I can't make this word out. Give it a try, will you?"

I held out the page to him and he promptly said, "Poiuytrewq. Why Will, isn't that word composed of all the letters on the top row of a typewriter keyboard when read from right to left?"

"Yes," I said, basking in her stolen beauty for the last time before it went up in smoke. Literally.

"That's odd," he said. "I'd almost think you suspected me of being Sir Qwertyuiop and were trying to banish me back to the 37th Dimension with a clever ruse. A very clever ruse, I might add."

I stared at her for a long moment. There hadn't been a puff of smoke. She hadn't said, "Awp!" and promptly vanished. She was still my beautiful Kar'En.

"Will," she said, her eyes growing wide, "you don't mean to

tell me that you actually thought…"

"It doesn't matter what I thought, baby," I said, nearly in tears. "I'm just an idiot. A crazy, insecure idiot."

"You certainly are," she snapped. And then she smiled. "But you're *my* crazy, insecure idiot!"

She wrapped me in her arms and it was springtime again. It was Friday afternoon and the school bell had rung. The Giants had won the pennant! The Giants had won the pennant!

We ate our *asado* in Buenos Aires that night, and afterward we walked the white beaches of the French Riviera. When it was time to part I held her so tight that had she been an ordinary girl, and not the second most powerful being in the universe, I surely would have cracked her ribs and ruptured her spleen.

But that was the last peace I knew that night. It took me hours to fall asleep, and then I slept fitfully. I had strange dreams, in which voices seemed to be calling to me from an unimaginable distance. They were telling me to let her go, let her go. I had no idea who the voices belonged to, but somehow I knew whom they bade me release. I knew they meant Kar'En.

In the morning I was exhausted but anxious, more anxious than I'd been the previous day. Before I'd finished breakfast I found myself rifling obsessively through my stacks of *Commotion Comics* again, my anxiety turning to panic. I reminded myself that she'd said "poiuytrewq" loud and clear, proving that I hadn't fallen in love with a maleficent fairy. But another voice was rising in my mind, asking a terrible question: Did that prove that she was really Kar'En?

After all, weren't there others who could impersonate the Girl of Splendor? Weren't impersonators a dime a dozen in the world of the Splendid Cousins?

Then I saw the comic that I had half-remembered from the day before, the one where the Cuckoo Splendid Girl comes to Earth—looking for her twisted version of romance!

I caught myself. I had no evidence for what I was thinking. And anyway, didn't the Cuckoos look like photographic negatives of Splendid Man and all his friends? My Kar'En hardly had black teeth and orange eyes. Of course, that was scarcely conclusive. Why couldn't the Cuckoo have disguised herself? Why couldn't she have worn one of those amazingly lifelike rubber masks that everybody in Splendid Man's world seem to have ready access to? Well, and amazingly lifelike leggings as well.

And then it suddenly made perfect, horrific sense.

The Cuckoos always do the opposite of what their Earthly originals do. If the Cuckoo Splendid Girl wanted to take the place of the real Splendid Girl from whom she had been imperfectly duplicated, she would have noted that Kar'En dated Splendid Heroes and rock stars and Oscar winners—but then, in the backwards way of all the Cuckoos, decided to date a no-account schmuck instead! And of course she would love me! If the real Splendid Girl had ever met me, I'm sure she wouldn't have *hated* me. She would have felt only a profound indifference to my underwhelming charms. And didn't Elie Wiesel say that the opposite of love is indifference?

I opened my window and vibrated the teeth of my SOS Comb.

"Hi, pal," Cal said, almost instantaneously.

"Hi, pal," I said. I noticed that Cal never asked what the emergency was anymore. I had abused the SOS Comb so many times that he'd come to take my summoning him for petty reasons for granted. "I hope I'm not interrupting anything," I added.

"You would have if you'd summoned me a second earlier," he said. "I just finished reading the thirty Philip K. Dick books you loaned me. Brrr, reality was putty in that man's hands!"

Yes, I thought, reality was indeed putty. I found myself wishing I'd loaned him thirty love stories instead.

"Tell me," I said. "Are there really imperfect Cuckoo duplicates of all your friends and loved ones in the Cuckoo World?"

"Why yes, Will," said Cal. "There's even one of you these days."

"You're kidding me," I said. "What's he like?"

"The usual. He's a negative version of you who prides himself on his pedestrian taste, utter lack of originality, and complete indifference to literary sensibilities."

I couldn't help chuckling. "And he's proud to be a total failure too, right?"

"Oh no," Cal said. "He's the Cuckoo World's best-selling novelist."

That didn't help my mood any, but I forged on. "So there's a Cuckoo Splendid Girl too? It's not just something they made up for the comics?"

"You know there's nothing made-up in the comics, Will. Why do you ask?"

I shrugged. "No particular reason."

He looked at me through narrowed eyes. "Now, Will," he said. "You aren't getting paranoid on me, are you? Yesterday you were worried about Sir Qwertyuiop and today it's the Cuckoo Splendid Girl. What gives?"

Was I getting paranoid? I wanted to think I was. I wanted to believe that this was all just cooked up in my own fear-addled brain. But the logic of my arguments was just so *compelling!*

"Gosh pal, it's nothing like that," I said. "I'm just...doing research for a story. A story about the Cuckoos. That's all."

He gave me a suspicious look and flew away.

Kar'En and I had made plans to get together after school. She fetched me at four sharp and flew us back to Axial Town at Splendid Speed. We strolled around the town square for a bit and then dropped in at the town's favorite teen hangout, Zany Zach's Malt Shoppe. I was struck by how successfully Axial Town had fended off the changing fashions of the past fifteen or twenty years. This felt more like being in a malt shoppe in the Turnipville of Splendid Boy's era than in any town in contemporary America. Which only reinforced what I'd been thinking all evening: Nothing in the world of the Splendid Heroes is what it seems!

Splendid Girl had changed into her frumpy Peggy Pearl Perkins identity so as not to attract attention, and we took our place at the counter. Tommy, the fullback on the Stantheman College football team, took our orders, a banana split for Peggy and a Coca Cola for me. A twist record played on the jukebox.

"Hey, daddy-o!" a teenaged voice called from somewhere behind us. "Dig that crazy platter!"

When our orders came, Peggy decided she'd rather sit in a booth and we moved to a vacant one. "What's the matter tonight, dearest?" she asked. "You seem jumpy or something. You're not thinking you'd rather be out with Anaïs Nin, are you?"

I almost said, "No. I'm thinking I'd rather be out with the *real* Peggy Pearl Perkins." But I bit my tongue. After all, I wasn't sure this was an impostor, was I? If this was the real Peggy Pearl, I had to let her prove herself to me.

And then it hit me. In the months we'd been together, she had accused me of wishing I was dating not only Anaïs Nin but Dorothy Parker, Jean Rhys, Alice B. Toklas, and Ayn Rand. Of course! A Cuckoo girl would do precisely the opposite of what a real girl would do—she wouldn't be jealous of living rivals, she'd be jealous of the dead! Did I need any more proof?

I snatched at her face to tear the mask from it, but apparently even the imperfect reflexes of a Cuckoo were quick enough for her to pull back before I could grab her.

"Will, what are you doing?" she gasped.

"You can quit pretending now," I said. "The jig is up. I've seen through your disguise. Or should I say, your amazingly lifelike rubber mask and leggings!"

She got up and ran from the malt shop. I noticed some of the clean-cut teens glare at me in anger as I took off in pursuit.

She was standing just outside the door, crying softly. "Oh, Will," she blubbered. "How could you? What if some of the gals and fellas had heard, and deduced that I wear a disguise to conceal the fact that I'm secretly Splendid Girl, the Princess of Power?"

"Oh, for God's sake!" I said. "Give it up!" And I grabbed her around the neck and started tugging furiously at the mask.

I'd just begun to consider the implications of the fact that her face wasn't tearing away in my hands as I'd expected, when I felt something like an anvil hit my back. I was hammered face-first into the pavement. When I rolled over I saw Tommy and Biff, the starting center on the squad, looming over me.

"Is he being mean to you, Peggy?" Biff barked.

"Oh no, fellas!" Peggy cried. "There's no problem, really!"

"No problem?" said Tommy. "You scram out of the malt shoppe with the waterworks flowing and then we catch this square trying to unscrew your noggin—and that's no problem?"

"It's all been a misunderstanding," Peggy insisted.

The boys reluctantly let me up. "If you say so," Biff said, and they left us alone.

Peggy was staring at me in fury. "You've got some explaining to do, buster!"

There was nothing for it but to come clean. Or partly clean. "I thought you were the Cuckoo Splendid Girl," I said. It sounded lame even to my ears.

"What?" she snapped. "You thought I was a crazy, mixed-up imperfect duplicate of myself?"

I nodded contritely.

"But...why?"

"Because you're always asking me if I wouldn't rather be with dead women writers," I said, sounding lamer and lamer. "Doesn't that sound like something a Cuckoo would do?"

"Why, of all the nerve," she railed at me. "So now I've got a backwards, retarded personality? Is that what you're saying?"

"No! I'm saying the Cuckoo impersonating you has a backwards, retarded personality!"

"But a Cuckoo *hasn't* been impersonating me, Mr. Jones! I happen to be the real me. Your real backwards, retarded girlfriend!"

She flew me home in a huff, and for the first time we parted in anger.

Whatever I'd been dating all this time was clever, I'd grant her that. Clever enough to try deflecting my suspicions by feigning anger. But there was no longer any doubt in my mind that I'd been going out with an impostor from the start. Would the real Splendid Girl date a guy who could fall for such an obvious hoax?

Oh, I'll admit she almost pulled it off. For one terrible moment I thought how sweet it would be to surrender to the old fantasy that

Splendid Girl loved me. But then I thought of the pain, disappointment, and humiliation that would follow once the truth was revealed—and I knew that I had to redirect all my thoughts back to exposing the impostor!

It took me a long time to fall asleep that night. My mind whirled frantically through all the possibilities of who the impostor might be. It could be a Splendid Girl robot gone haywire. Or a Splendid Girl from the far future attempting to alter the course of history (vainly, of course) by changing events in the past. Or even a life-like construct generated by those Pipe-Dream Fish from Aldebaran in Splendid Man's interplanetary menagerie. But before I finally drifted off I was pretty sure I'd figured out who the real culprit was. It could only be one of the members of the Splendid Girl Calamity Unit, those tiny Splendid Girl lookalikes who hailed from Strontor, the City in a Can!

Why couldn't one of the Calamity Girls have noticed me on my trip to Strontor and developed a crush on me? Granted, it didn't seem very likely, but I could imagine a sheltered, germ-sized gal who hardly ever saw men from the outside world falling for the likes of me. It made a lot more sense than imagining that the real Splendid Girl could have!

And why couldn't she have gotten her hands on the exchange ray developed by the renegade Strontorian I'd read about in that comic book the other day? What else would she do but use it to take Splendid Girl's place on Earth…while the real Splendid Girl was probably locked up or drugged somewhere. Or, more likely still, hypnotized or given amnesia and made to take her evil lookalike's place so that no one would notice a missing Calamity Girl!

I was momentarily filled with rage at the thought of my beloved Kar'En trapped unaware in Strontor, her own life stolen from her, until I remembered that I had never actually *met* Kar'En. My beloved, in fact, was the very Calamity Girl who had stolen her life. Which, when I thought about it, wasn't necessarily such a terrible thing. After all, if I really had been dating a Calamity Girl all this time, what was not to like? She was just as lovely as the real article, just as powerful under Earth's argon-tinged atmosphere and lesser gravity, and possessed of a sweet, pleasant personality. And better yet, she hadn't dated every prize catch in the universe!

Then I shook my head in disgust. What the hell was wrong with me? How could I think such a thing? As wonderful as she might seem, the Calamity Girl was a kidnapper. And the real Splendid Girl was her prisoner. Like it or not, I had to expose the girl I loved—in order to free the girl I'd only thought I loved!

The pseudo-Kar'En and I hadn't made any plans for our next date, so when she dropped in the following evening I suggested a visit to Strontor, the City in a Can.

She was bit subdued. I suppose she was still peeved at me from our last date. Even a kidnapper and impostor would probably be offended at being mistaken for a Cuckoo in a rubber mask. But at the mention of Strontor a flame kindled in her eyes.

"I see," she said. "You want to see that Jen'Ee."

"Who?" I said.

"Don't you dare play innocent with me, Will Jones! Splendid Man told me all about your infatuation with that little minx who bears an uncanny resemblance to your ex-fiancée!"

"But sugar," I said, "she isn't a writer."

That seemed to appease her. "Okay," she agreed. "Now that I think about it, I haven't visited Strontor in ages."

So she wrapped me in her cape and we zoomed to the moon. Once inside the Citadel she hooked me up to that language-teaching thingamajig, outfitted both of us with parachutes, and subjected us to the shrink ray. This time, when we flew to the top of the can, we discovered that Strontor's artificial sun *was* in our line of descent, and so we'd have to wait an hour before we could parachute down safely.

We snuggled together on top of the can and pretty soon we were smooching. It was nice to think that those luscious lips weren't the ones that had kissed Finwad or Robert Redford or Richard Roundtree or any other ultrafamous male you could think of. And once again I found myself wondering if I shouldn't leave well enough alone. After all, this girl really could love me. And why not? She was in reality a microbe that lived in a can, not the idol of billions.

"Okay" she said. "It's safe to go in now."

I realized that this was my last chance to hold on to her, but I kept mum. What would Splendid Man think of me if he should ever learn that I had known of his beloved cousin's imprisonment and done nothing to free her?

A welcoming committee showed up when we landed and once again I was fitted with special gravity shoes that enabled me to withstand Strontor's terrible gravitational pull. There was no sign of Jen'Ee this time, thank God!

We went for a stroll. I spotted dead ringers for Peter Frampton, Margaret Thatcher, and Louis-Ferdinand Céline.

"Anything in particular you'd like to do, Will?" she asked.

"Now that you mention it," I said, "I'd love to meet the Splendid Girl Calamity Unit, those miniature marvels who, gaining Splendid Powers under Earth's argon-tinged atmosphere and lesser gravity, have often come to your aid."

She touched something on her chest emblem, and within minutes we were surrounded by a gaggle of girls bearing a striking resemblance to Kar'En. Counting them quickly, I saw that there were twenty-four of them, the full roster of the Calamity Unit. That meant that the real Kar'En wasn't locked up anywhere but must be among these girls. While they chatted gaily, I looked around until I spotted the one who was Kar'En's exact double.

I sidled up to her and whispered, "Don't worry, Kar'En! I've come to get you out of here!"

She looked embarrassed. "I'm afraid you're mistaking me for..."

"We've got to get you back to your real life," I hissed. "The people of Earth need you!"

Now she looked uncomfortable. "I'm sorry," she said, "but I have no idea what you're talking about."

Another of my suspicions proven! The fiends *had* given her amnesia!

"Don't be afraid, Kar'En," I said. "They've no doubt given you false memory implants to make you think you're a member of..."

"Will?" I heard the impostor say behind me, and not with a pleasant tone. "What are you doing?"

"What am I doing?" I snapped, turning triumphantly on her. "I'm proving that the real Kar'En here..."

"Co'Ket," said the girl. "My name is Co'Ket."

"I'm proving that this poor girl who's been tricked into believing she's a Strontorian named Co'Ket..."

"Will," said the girl I'd parachuted down with. "Don't do this. Please."

"Think!" I shouted to the real Kar'En. "Haven't you ever wondered why you have strange memories, as if you'd grown up on a generation starship?"

The amnesiac girl turned, ironically, to the impostor who had replaced her, and said, "I think this would be a good time for me to go."

"I can prove it!" I screamed. "Show me her dental records!"

Well, to make a long story short, they did indeed produce her dental records, and then her fingerprints, and then some Strontorian gadget that reads the individual patterns in brain waves, and Co'Ket turned out to be exactly who she claimed to be.

The impostor didn't say a word as she escorted me out of Strontor and flew me back toward San Francisco. The depths of outer space could not have been any more silent than the creature I had thought was Splendid Girl. Which was fine with me, because it gave me time to think about what clever ruses might expose a rogue robot.

When we arrived at my apartment, I was surprised to find Splendid Man there waiting for us.

"Thank God you're here!" I said to him. "You can take care of this a lot easier than I could." I pointed at the impostor. "Quick, get her to tell you what she did with Splendid Girl before she tries to get away!"

But Splendid Man didn't budge. Instead, he and the impostor exchanged a troubled glance.

"See what I mean?" the impostor said.

Splendid Man turned back to me and fixed me with a gaze every bit as intense as the one to which Catman had subjected me. "The X-ray setting of my Splendid Vision reveals that he's not a robot," he said.

"Nor does mine show that he's the Cuckoo Will," said the impostor.

"What the hell?" I said. "I'm not the impostor! She is!"

Splendid Man indicated my typewriter. "Step over here, you," he said.

I was confused for a moment, and then it dawned on me. Not only had the phony Splendid Girl summoned Splendid Men via ventriloquism to meet us at my apartment, but she had also turned the tables on me and convinced him that *I* was the impostor! "My God," I said. "You can't really believe I'm Sir Qwertyuiop!"

"If you aren't," said Splendid Man, "you won't mind reading the top row from right to left."

I appealed to the impostor, but she looked just as stern as he did. I walked over and read off the letters. I even threw in the brackets and the tab for good measure. "See?" I said. "Still here."

"Then I don't know what to think," Splendid Man said.

"While I was in Strontor I confirmed that Will's Strontorian double is present and accounted for," the impostor said.

"Speak!" Splendid Man said, spearing me with an implacable glance. "Just who or what are you? And what have you done to the real Will Jones?"

I let myself fall back on my couch, horrified, numb, and humiliated. It had taken me a while, it had taken me far longer than I wanted to admit, but now it was finally sinking in. The most terrifying truth of all. I was really, truly engaged to the most desirable girl on the face of the earth.

"Okay," I said. "You can both stop. I've learned my lesson."

"Have you, Will?" asked Splendid Man.

When I gave my answer, I couldn't lift my eyes from the floor. "I guess I just can't believe that Splendid Girl, the Gal of Gloriousness, the idol of trillions, could ever love a nobody like me. I found it so hard to believe, in fact, that I convinced myself that only somebody or something pretending to be Splendid Girl could love me, or pretend to love me, as the case might be."

A silence followed. I still couldn't bring myself to make eye contact with either of them. Finally, Splendid Man cleared his throat and said, "Maybe I should leave you two alone."

"I'm sorry," I said.

"I'm not the one you need to apologize to," he said, and then I heard a whoosh.

I finally found the strength to lift my eyes. Splendid Girl was standing in the middle of the room, staring coldly at me. Neither of us spoke.

After a moment I patted the seat beside me and she came and sat. The silence wore on. At last I reached over and took her hand in mine.

"I love you," I said.

She looked me in the eye. "Would it do any good to say that I love you, too?"

"You don't have to," I said. "If you can still say it and mean it, though, I'd love to hear it."

"You won't think I'm an illusion projected by Mesmer Miss of the Array of Splendid Striplings?"

Mesmer Miss! I'd forgotten about her! I turned on Splendid Girl in alarm...but when I saw the anger in her eyes I felt myself wither in shame.

"Sorry," I said. "This is difficult for a guy like me."

"I love you, Will," she said.

I put my arms around her. For a moment she remained tense, but then she relaxed, and I held her tightly.

"Jeepers," I heard her sigh. But I couldn't tell if she sighed with relief or pleasure or dread, or a bit of all three.

Episode Fifteen
Who Knows What Tomorrow Will Bring?

I wanted a small ceremony, with a justice of the peace, just our folks as witnesses, and Cal, of course, to stand up for me. She wanted a gala affair with a guest list that included all the members of the Array of Splendid Striplings, the North American Alliance for Meetness, and the Pubescent Paladins. Not to mention all of Ken Clayton's friends and the entire populace of Strontor, the City in a Can. I was surprised she didn't insist on inviting Giganto the Splendid Mandrill.

I wanted to marry Peggy Pearl Perkins as myself, Will Jones, but she wanted the headlines to scream, LITERARY LAD WEDS SPLENDID GIRL! I would have been just as happy to settle down in my beloved Richmond District, or in bucolic Axial Town, maybe taking up Mr. Perkins on his offer to work at his engineering firm until I made my name as a writer, but Kar'En had her heart set on Beverly Hills. Not that she expected me to be able to afford it any time soon, but I guess she had faith in my literary future.

"Oooo, wouldn't you just love to live there?!" she squealed.

We were strolling along Hillcrest Road, and she was indicating another Ottoman-Tudor-Beaux-Arts monstrosity.

"I think Larry Storch lived there," I said.

"Who?"

"Doesn't matter," I said. "You know, I spotted some nice bungalows when we flew over Glendale."

"Jeepers!" she exclaimed. "Give the eyeball to that palace!"

"Those are Lance DeWilde's digs," I said.

"How do you know all this?" she asked,

"*People Magazine*," I said. "Never miss an issue."

"I wonder if they'll ever make a movie about me," she said.

"Better hope not," I said.

"Who do you think they'd get to play me?"

"There isn't anybody pretty enough," I said.

"Oh, Will! That was so sweet!" she cried. "Kiss me!"

I kissed her.

"Who do you think they'd get to play you?" she asked.

"Someone dashing, intelligent, mature..."

"I think Alan Alda would be good."

"For God's sake!" I said. "He must be pushing fifty! People were tired of him before I could write!"

"Golly!" she squealed. "Look at that one!"

"Built by Cantinflas in 1959," I said.

"Oh. What's this?"

I looked where she indicated, and saw what looked like a fist-sized jewel in a clump of azaleas. My first thought was that some drunken actress had dropped the hideous pendant she'd borrowed for the Oscars, but then Kar'En cried out, "Oh, no! I feel a strange tingling!" With a pang of horror, I realized that we'd stumbled upon some lavender strontiumite!

What bizarre, ghastly effect would it have on her? I wondered. Would she grow incredibly tall and become the Skyscraper Splendid Girl? Would she develop amnesia or multiple personalities? Would her voice metamorphose into Truman Capote's? Even knowing that the effects of lavender strontiumite wear off after forty-eight hours, I still shuddered at the possibilities.

"Speak to me, darling!" I gasped.

"Do I look funny?" she asked. "Have I grown a mustache or sprouted a zit or developed gills?"

"No," I reassured her. "You look just like yourself."

"Then how...?"

But she never got to finish the sentence, because suddenly she'd vanished into thin air!

I whipped out my SOS comb...and stopped myself from vibrating the teeth just in time! What was I thinking? Had I summoned Splendid Man, he would have been affected by the lavender strontiumite in the same way, and vanished God knows where!

I broke into a run and didn't stop until I'd covered several blocks. I didn't know exactly how far from the malevolent rays of the strontiumite Splendid Man needed to be to remain unaffected, but I figured I'd come far enough. Quickly I vibrated the teeth.

"What it is, Will?" Splendid Man asked, wafting to the ground beside me an instant later. "You look as if you've seen a ghost."

"It's Splendid Girl!" I blurted, and proceeded to tell him what had happened.

His brow furrowed. "Where exactly is this strontiumite?" he asked.

I told him, and he took me under his arm and we shot into the sky. It took me a while to orient myself from the air, but finally I recognized the Cantinflas mansion, and Splendid Man used the telescopic setting of his Splendid Vision to study the chunk of shining rock.

"Oh, my," he said, and zoomed straight toward it.

"Are you crazy?" I yelled. "Do you want to disappear, too?"

"Not to worry, Will," he said, coming to ground next to the azaleas. "I recognize this specimen, because I've been affected by it in the past. And, as you know, a single meteor of lavender strontiumite cannot affect a native of Strontium twice." He bent down and picked it up.

"Well, don't leave me in suspense!" I cried. "How did it affect you?"

"It sent me five years into the future. Only I didn't know I was in the future. For the forty-eight hours I was there, I thought that's where I belonged."

"So tell me," I said, with bated breath. "Did the Giants finally win a World Series?"

"I couldn't say, Will. I was affected by this rock seven years ago, so I spent forty-eight hours in 1980."

"So you figure Kar'En is in 1987 as we speak?"

"No question about it."

"Really? Lavender strontiumite always affects Strontiumese in the exact same way?"

"Always. Once, the same chunk of lavender strontiumite turned both Kar'En and myself into a Splendid Humpty-Dumpty Man *and* Girl, respectively. Another time, it reversed both of our sexual orientations."

That one got to me. It was one thing to imagine Splendid Girl looking like a human egg, but quite another to think of her as a lesbian!

"Really?" I gulped. "And did Kar'En...did she...you know...date any..."

"Billie Jean King," Splendid Man said.

I mulled that over for a while. Then it hit me. "Wow. It must have been strange for you, Cal. Being gay for forty-eight hours, I mean."

Splendid Man fixed me with one of his odd looks. "I'd rather not talk about it, Will."

"I understand, pal," I said. "I don't imagine I would either. So what do we do now? Shall we fly into the future and try to find Kar'En?"

"I'm afraid it wouldn't do any good," said Splendid Man. "As she'll believe she's where she belongs, she'll just think we're crazy if we try to tell her otherwise. No, I'm afraid you've got no choice but to wait for 10:46 AM the day after tomorrow."

But it turned out he was wrong. He had no sooner dropped me off at my apartment than I heard a window open and Splendid Girl zoomed into the room. "Kar'En!" I cried. "What are you doing here?"

"For Pete's sake," she said forlornly. "I'm the one who should be asking you that. I don't know how you managed to flee into the past again, and frankly I don't care anymore, but you must be insane to come here. What if you ran into your 1982 self? Don't you know what a time-paradox that could create?"

"Huh?" I said.

"And besides, I don't know why you want to keep going back to the time you were stuck in the worst temporary job of your life, binding turkey legs together with those little metal doodads!"

"Are you telling me...?" I started, but that's as far as I got. Splendid Girl had thrown her cape around me and in the next instant I could feel us flying at faster-than-light speed. And that's when I realized what was going on. This wasn't *my* Kar'En, but the Kar'En who had been catapulted into the future and who for forty-eight hours would firmly believe that that's where she belonged! But why had she retrieved me from the past? Had something happened to the Will Jones of her time? A moment later we came to earth and I peeked out from under the folds of the cape.

We were in small park that I didn't recognize. "Where are we?" I asked.

"Oh, don't be tiresome," was all she would say, and proceeded to change from her Splendid Costume into her secret identity of Peggy Pearl Perkins. Only when the change was complete could I see that she didn't resemble the Peggy I knew at all. Her hair was dyed red and held flat by a headband, and she was wearing an old pair of jeans and a shapeless sweatshirt.

"Peggy, what...?" I asked.

She had turned on her heel and was striding out of the park. After a moment's hesitation I followed. When we emerged from the park I saw that we were in a bleak, treeless neighborhood of shabby apartment buildings. Peggy led me to the entrance of one of them, but before going in she stopped at the mailboxes and opened one with a label reading *Wayne & Patty Smith.*

"What are you doing?!" I gasped. "Don't you know it's a federal offense to steal someone else's mail?!"

She gave me a withering look and moved into the dingy lobby that smelled of old cabbage. In utter confusion I followed her down a hallway that now smelled more like moldy broccoli until we came to a door. The number on the door bore the same number as the mailbox she'd raided. When Peggy opened the door and walked straight in like she lived there I started to get really scared. But all I could do was follow her inside.

I'd thought my apartment in the Richmond district of San Francisco was dumpy, but this place made it look like something out of *Metropolitan Home*. The furniture—what little there was of it—was old and decrepit, the carpet was threadbare and needed vacuuming, the...but you get the picture. The Smiths, whoever they were, weren't doing very well for themselves.

But then I saw something that almost stopped my heart. That old, battered, twelve-inch Zenith—it was the TV set I owned at this very minute in the past! I started looking around and spotted more familiar items. The rocking chair that didn't rock anymore. The couch I'd inherited from my parents. My beloved bookshelves, but now pitifully denuded of books. And it became suddenly, horribly clear just who these Smiths really were.

Peggy—or Patty—had gone straight into the bedroom. Now she came back into the living room where I still stood like a statue, and I saw that she'd changed into a coffee-stained work shirt, waitress's apron, and bulbous white comfort shoes. Without giving me a glance, she picked up a purse and started for the door.

"Where are you going?" I asked.

"Where do you think I'm going? Am I supposed to quit my job at Pete's Eats or something? Are you suddenly able to support us on what you make at your never-ending series of temporary jobs? Or did you finally sell one of your books and forget to tell me? Hell, if you could sell just a *short story* we could afford to turn the cable back on. But I know how it is. Art before commerce. Mustn't sully the purity of your craft."

"Jesus," I muttered.

She reached for the doorknob, but then changed her mind and faced me again. "Don't forget that my parents invited us over for dinner tonight, and that Kev'In doesn't like it when we're late. Do you understand? I won't be humiliated again."

"Kev'In?" I asked.

But she'd already left.

So, the Will of the future was apparently in the habit of running off. He'd probably taken a run-out powder just recently, and Kar'En had somehow gotten it into her head that he'd escaped into the past and accidentally brought the 1982 me here. But what if the Will of 1987 should return while I was still around? Would one of those dread time paradoxes occur? There was nothing I could do about that, though, so I shoved it out of my mind and decided to explore the apartment.

There was a dingy kitchen and a tiny bathroom and a single bedroom. The latter was appointed even more shabbily than the living room. I started going through the drawers of a battered bureau. There, under a pile of Peggy's underclothes, I found what I'd half expected to find.

It was a newspaper clipping, folded into a tiny square. I carefully unfolded it and read the article with a sinking heart. It seems that in 1983 I—or, more properly, the Will Jones who existed in this future—had been kidnapped by the she-android Cerebria, Splendid Girl's archnemesis. Under the influence of her truth serum I had revealed Splendid Girl's identity, and Cerebria had shouted it to the world.

So that explained the Smith business. Because of me, Kar'En had had to abandon her Peggy Pearl Perkins identity and assume a new secret identity. And I, as her husband, had had to change my name as well. And this town we lived in was no doubt located far from any of our previous haunts, away from friends or family or even casual acquaintances who might have recognized us. It appeared we were utterly alone in the world. And that's when I saw the letter.

It was in the same drawer in which I'd found the newspaper clipping, and as it was addressed to both Wayne and Patty, I didn't feel too badly about taking a peek at it. I drew the letter out of the envelope and read:

Dear Wi...er...Wayne and Peg...er...Patty,
Although I fully understand that you had to relocate your father and I after Wi...er...Wayne inadvertently revealed your secret identity to the world, in order to prevent your enemies, like Pixie Pascal or the Vengeance Is Mine Squad, from exacting revenge on you through your loved ones—in this case your loving foster parents—I do wish you could have picked a town a little less remote than Ice Cape,

Alaska. Not to mention one a little less cold. And to make matters worse, they don't need engineers here, so your father could only find gainful employment in the whale-blubber plant. Oh, dear. But I suppose I should be grateful for our lives, although I must admit it's difficult sometimes. In fact, sometimes I wish we were dead and in the ground. But no, dear foster daughter and son, I don't really mean that. The Aurora Borealis is awfully nice, even though we only see it once in a blue moon. And our Eskimo neighbors are very friendly. After their own fashion, that is. Well, that's all I have for now as, frankly, there isn't much to report from up here. Hope this finds you well. Or, at least, better than us.

Love,

Ir...er...Inez and Te...er...Fred

So if it wasn't enough that I'd ruined Kar'En's life, I'd destroyed her foster parents' as well! But then I remembered that when she'd mentioned her father, she'd called him neither Ted nor Fred, but Kev'In.

I figured it was hopeless, but I whipped out my SOS comb and thrummed the teeth anyway. As it turned out, I figured wrong. An instant later Splendid Man was tapping at the bedroom window.

"Is it you?" I said, when I'd let him in. "Or the you of 1987?"

"It's me, Will," he said. "The Splendid Man of 1982. The one from this reality is probably off on a space mission, and hence unable to answer your summons."

"That's amazing!" I said. "I didn't think the signal could reach you across the temporal barrier."

"It couldn't, of course. But it just so happened that my comrade in the North American Alliance for Meetness, the Mexican Manhunter, was on a case in the future and spotted you with his telescopic vision just when you vibrated the teeth of the comb, and relayed the summons to me via the NAAFM emergency signaling device."

"That's one hell of a coincidence," I said.

He shrugged. "Coincidences happen."

I explained everything that had occurred since I'd last seen him. And then I asked him the million-dollar question. "Tell me, pal. Did the future your 1975 self visited in 1980 turn out to be true?"

"Not entirely, Will. There were actually several differences. Jimmy Carter's mission to rescue the Iran hostages was successful, and he won reelection in a landslide."

"Oh, wow! That's great! And how fared the country in Carter's second term?"

"I wouldn't know, Will. A week after the election he was eaten by the Hideous Thing from 1,000,000 A.D.. But why do you ask?"

"Look around, pal. If the future was set in stone, this is what Kar'En and I would have to look forward to. Not exactly Beverly Hills, is it?" Then I explained about having exposed her secret identity, to boot.

"That is indeed grim, Will."

"And that's not the half of it. I still haven't sold any of my writing, and poor Kar'En is a waitress at a place called Pete's Eats in her secret identity. And let me tell you, she doesn't seem to be very happy!"

"I'm sad to hear it."

But then I remembered Kev'In, and I told Splendid Man about Kar'En's parents who we were supposed to have dinner with that night. "But how can that be?" I asked. "Kar'En's real parents, Kev'In and Kath'Ee, died on the generation starship that brought Splendid Girl to Earth."

Splendid Man's brow furrowed. "Have I ever mentioned the Region of the Not Really Dead, Will?"

"Say what?"

"I guess I haven't," he said. "The comics have shied away from mentioning it as well, probably because of the religious connotations. But we Strontiumese have long suspected the existence of another dimension containing billions of souls who only *seem* to have died in great cataclysms."

"Are you telling me that Kar'En's parents are still alive?" I asked. "Or, to put it more exactly, not *really* dead? I thought you told me she was the only survivor on that generation starship!"

"I thought you knew I meant the only regular-sized physical survivor in our dimension," Cal said. "That's generally what we Strontiumese mean by 'only survivor,' which is why the comics and movies often refer to me as the 'sole survivor of an inundated planet,' or, 'the last scion of Strontium.' Actually, if you count Ghost World, Strontor, the City in a Can, and the Region of the Not Really Dead, pretty much the whole population is still around."

"Then you're saying that they must have found some way to pass from this weird region into our reality? Or at least into the reality of this alternate future?"

"Apparently so, Will."

"This gets wackier and wackier," I said. And suddenly I felt like I couldn't take it anymore. "Take me home, Splendid Man! Take me away from this horrible place!"

"I'm afraid that wouldn't do any good, Will. As Splendid Girl seems determined that you attend the dinner at her parents' house tonight, there probably isn't any place or time to which I could whisk you that she wouldn't be able to find you. I'm afraid you're stuck here for another forty-four hours, thirteen minutes, and nineteen seconds, give or take a few nanoseconds."

"But what if the Will from this era shows up? Won't that cause some ghastly time-paradox?"

"Yes, indeed. But I already searched for this reality's Will with the telescopic setting of my Splendid Vision, and I located him at a YMCA in Broken Bow, Nebraska. It's not at all likely that he could make it back here before the deadline, even if he took a mind to."

"Where is here, anyway?"

"Broken Arrow, Oklahoma. Your future self seems to have an attraction to towns named after broken symbols of masculinity."

"Good God," I said. "Can they really be so miserable that my counterpart prefers to live in a YMCA than with his lovely bride? It's too horrible for words!"

Splendid Man only looked uncomfortable.

"But it doesn't have to be this way, does it, pal? You said yourself that the future isn't set in stone, right? Maybe when Kar'En and I get married our lives won't turn out like this at all!"

"Maybe not," he said, but he didn't say it with a lot of conviction.

He soon left, and I stayed. And that night Kar'En and I went to her real parents' house for dinner, and it was as dreadful as I'd feared. Although Kev'In and Kath'Ee tried to hide it, it was clear that they loathed me and held me responsible for their daughter's sad state of affairs. To make matters worse, when you looked at them in a certain light, you could actually see right through them! But the worst came at the very end, when Kev'In looked me in the eyes and said, "We may be fated to remain the Not Really Dead, Will. But thanks to you, our little girl is trapped forever among the Not Really Alive." Kar'En sobbed all the way home.

I slept alone on the couch that night. She left for work without a word the next morning, and I hung around the house doing nothing. It turned out that this Will was temporarily between temporary jobs at the moment, so there was nowhere I had to be. I searched the apartment again, for lack of anything better to do, and found a couple of manuscripts I didn't recognize. One was a literary fable about a peasant whose life is ruined when he falls in love with a goddess that looked like it was striving to be some kind of metaphor. The other was a horror novel about a New England town being menaced by a feral cat. Neither felt like anything I had any business writing. Not surprisingly, appended to each was a thick bundle of rejection slips.

I spent the rest of the day tidying the place up. To judge by the look of surprise on Kar'En's face when she got home, the Will of this reality must not have been much of a housekeeper. She seemed to thaw a little for a while, but it didn't last. The drabness of their lives descended upon our shoulders all too soon, and shortly after dinner she once more vanished into the bedroom, not to emerge again for the rest of the night.

The next morning she left for work without even saying

goodbye. I looked around the house wondering if there was anything I could do to make it just a tiny bit less dismal and my eyes fell upon the digital clock on the kitchen counter. It was 10:47 AM! The forty-eight hours had elapsed! Kar'En must have been whisked back into the past—and yet here I was, still in 1987!

I panicked. She must have abandoned me in this dismal future, I thought. And who could blame her? I could easily imagine her getting back to 1982 and regaining her senses as the effects of the lavender strontiumite wore off, then deciding she was much better off marooning me in the future where I wouldn't be able to wreck her life.

Then, suddenly, I saw her flying through a window. For a horrifying moment I couldn't tell which Splendid Girl I was seeing. It only made sense that it was the Splendid Girl of the past, come to retrieve me, but she looked so terribly sad that I couldn't help but doubt my senses. Before I could speak, she was wrapping me in her cape. Within instants we were attaining faster-than-light velocity.

And no sooner had we set foot in my apartment back in 1982 than she broke into sobs. "Oh, Will," she cried. "Can you ever forgive me for making you so miserable?"

My heart sank. Although it was clearly *I* who had ruined *her* life in the future, the goodness of her soul would not allow her to shift the blame. It was more than I could take.

I opened my mouth to speak, then hesitated. Hadn't Splendid Man told me that the future, unlike the past, was not written in stone? But I knew it was no good. I knew that the future I'd spent forty-four hours in was far likelier to come true than Jimmy Carter being reelected, and that Kar'En, rather than getting the Beverly Hills mansion of her dreams, would wind up in a dump in Broken Arrow, Oklahoma.

It broke my heart, but I did the only thing left to do. I tilted her head back with my forefinger and gazed into her limpid blue eyes. Then I said the only words I could possibly say and still retain a shred of self-respect.

•••

When Splendid Man took the half-empty highball glass from my hand, I realized I'd nodded off. We'd been drinking steadily for hours, but I hardly felt the effects. And no, I hadn't developed invulnerable brain cells. I'd never felt more vulnerable in my life.

"Time is it?" I asked.

"Three A.M.," he said. "Which reminds me of that quote of F. Scott Fitzgerald's you told me. 'In a real dark night of the soul…'"

"It's okay, pal," I said. "I don't feel like talking about Fitzgerald now."

"Sure, pal," he said.

We were silent for a while. Then I lit a cigarette and said, "I guess I was right last month, when I had my paranoid fugue. Splendid Girl never really loved me."

"What are you talking about?" he said.

I shrugged. "She didn't even argue with me," I said. "She just let me break up with her without putting up a fight at all."

"That's not fair, Will. You're failing to take into account your own remarkable powers of persuasion. That and the fact that your reasons for breaking up with her were pretty hard to argue with."

"Yeah," I said. "How could she ever have been happy with me, anyway? God, she had everything. Power. Beauty. Goodness. Those sparkling eyes. That golden hair. Those little red boots. The way you could see her panties when she flew…."

Cal cleared his throat loudly. "Let me tell you something, Will. It's high time you stopped selling yourself short. You're a kind, charming, wonderful guy. Truth to tell, I would have been shocked if Splendid Girl *hadn't* fallen in love with you. And having won her love, you had the courage to make the right decision and let her go. That was big, Will. That was heroic."

I nodded. "Thanks, pal."

"And don't go telling yourself that this was your only shot at happiness. Who knows what tomorrow will bring?"

Before long I felt myself starting to nod off again. I heard Splendid Man rise to his feet, and I opened my eyes. He was standing by an open window, preparing to take flight.

"Will you be all right now, Will?" he asked.

"Sure, pal. Thanks for staying with me."

"Anything for a pal, pal." Again he appeared ready to leave, but then he turned and said, "Let me tell you something else, Will. I was there when the Array of Splendid Striplings received you into their glorious ranks. I was there when the North American Alliance for Meetness, the greatest gathering of heroes in the universe, voted you in as their mascot. But I've never been so proud of you as I am today. Today you've proved yourself a splendid man."

"For God's sake," I said, "get out of here before you make me start bawling."

He smiled at me and rose into the sky.

•••

The next month I broke down and bought an issue of *Commotion Comics, Featuring Splendid Girl.* I flipped it open with my heart in my throat—and there I was in the opening scene! I, Will Jones, appearing in a comic book! They drew me looking a little geekier than I thought was accurate, but still. The scene showed me breaking up with Splendid Girl. I came off pretty harsh in the dialogue, but there was one panel in which I actually looked handsome, if somewhat stern and uncompromising. All in all, I could live with the trade-off.

The rest of the comic was about Splendid Girl, having decided her heart was permanently broken, leaving home and entering a convent. She was still able to sneak out and fight crime a lot, and she soon became known as the Flying Carmelite Nun.

Another month passed, and I discovered that that phase of her life hadn't lasted any longer than the others, as in the very next issue I found her renouncing her vows as she confronted a new villain called the Repartee-er, who could only be defeated with clever verbal jabs. (Which must have come as a great relief to Sid Sidman, the long-time scripter of her comic-book stories, as the whole Carmelite thing had seriously limited her dialogue.)

And then in the third issue I bought she met some goon named the Erector from out Cassiopeia way. When they started smooching on page eight the comic book bounced off my wall.

I had to get out of the house. After three months I thought I might be getting over her, but there I was bleeding from the heart again. I remembered that I was down to my last ten or twelve packages of Instant Ramen and figured a trip to Albertson's might distract me a little.

And that's where I saw her. Raven-haired and olive-skinned, as exotic as could be. She looked Middle Eastern, I thought, or maybe Greek. I thought of lamb and feta cheese and…well, of Greek things. When she stopped by the tomato display I sidled over and asked if she knew how to pick the ripe ones. She responded in a totally unintelligible language.

I reached for my SOS Comb.

Episode Sixteen
To the Ends of the Universe

I woke up happy. It was Saturday morning, and I'd just proudly handed in my resignation from my temporary job driving a good humor truck. I was in the mood for an outing. Maybe even someplace far, like Glen Ellen or Monterey. I was trying to make up my mind whether I'd rather spend the day hiking around Jack London's old turf or eating calamari in Steinbeck country, when I heard a tapping at my window.

As my apartment is on the second floor, it didn't take a rocket scientist to figure out it was Splendid Man. Sure enough, he was hovering just outside. I threw open the window and he wafted in.

"Hi, pal," I said.

"Hi, pal," he said. "How'd you like to go on a little trip today?"

"Why, that's amazing!" I said. "I was planning on the very thing myself. I just can't decide between Glen Ellen and Monterey. Or are they too far away for you?"

"Actually, Will," he said. "I was thinking of going a little farther than that."

"Where to?" I asked. "San Diego? Shasta?"

"I was thinking to the ends of the universe."

"Well, that sounds like…huh?!"

"I just finished reading the copy of *On the Nature of Things* by Lucretius that you loaned me. Remember where he asks if a man went to the 'last limits' of space and hurled a spear, would the spear bounce off or keep on going? That really seized my imagination, Will, and I'd like to learn the answer. Game?"

"Hell, yes!" I said. "Shall I pack a suitcase?"

"Oh, no. I'm sure we can make it home for dinner. Maybe you could make us some sandwiches for lunch."

"Will do."

"While you do that," he said, "I'll go build us a spaceship."

We both finished our tasks at the same time.

"Ready, pal?" Splendid Man said.

"Always ready for adventure, pal!"

We flew to where he'd parked the spaceship in Golden Gate Park. It looked like a big goldfish bowl with a couple of chairs rigged up on gyros inside. "Where's the engine?" I asked.

"There isn't one," he said. "I'll be supplying the motive power, as no known engine in the universe could give us the speed we require. If we expect to be home in time for dinner, that is."

He took us up slowly so that the G's wouldn't kill me, then gradually picked up speed. I was shocked to see Saturn loom up ahead almost instantly.

"What happened to Mars and Jupiter?" I said.

"Their orbits aren't aligned with that of the ringed planet," Cal explained.

"Is Pluto's?" I said. "I want to see what the outermost planet in our Solar System looks like."

"I don't believe it is, Will. But it's a moot point, anyway. We're in interstellar space already."

He was stretched out full length in our little bowl, apparently pushing the ship along with his outstretched arms. That was some pushing, I tell you!

"Do you have any idea how far we'll be traveling, Cal? I mean, how big is the universe anyway?"

"You mean the observable universe, don't you Will? Because all we can ever measure is that which we can see. Scientists have measured the observable universe at thirteen-point-seven billion light years in radius. I know that to be wrong, because the telescopic setting of my Splendid Vision can see a tad over fifteen billion light years and, with every parsec we're traveling now, I can see more universe ahead."

"Wow," I said. "I'm glad I made big sandwiches."

He shot me a glance. "This is the life, eh, pal? Adventuring together again! Just like old times!"

I patted him on the back. "You said it, pal!"

He noticed something over my shoulder. "Look over to your right, Will. And down about twelve-point-three degrees. See that sun with the bluish tinge?"

I spotted it, but we were moving so fast now that it was quickly lost behind us.

"What about it?" I asked.

"That was the parent sun of the planet on which I've often imprisoned Cerebriac. I made it quite escape-proof, if I say so myself. He's only managed to bust loose a dozen times."

"Huh? How can you call that escape-proof?"

"I mean it relatively, of course. Pox Pascal has escaped maximum security penitentiaries hundreds of times."

We zoomed past a spiral nebula, a crab nebula, and a black hole. If you've never seen a black hole, you're not missing much. It's black. And it's a hole. I understand they exert a terrible gravitational pull, but if this one yanked Splendid Man off course by so much as a millimeter, you wouldn't know it by me. I guess being from a heavy-gravity planet has its perks.

A while later he pointed out a pinkish sun. Although it didn't look like a sun anymore. We had reached such unbelievable velocities that the suns looked more like dashes than dots now. "That sun is orbited by an Earth-like planet, but with an argon-free atmosphere," he explained, "which, as you know, causes me to lose all my Splendid Powers, and once I was lured there by the Vengeance Is Mine Squad, those galaxy-spanning criminals who are always seeking to avenge themselves for previous defeats at my hands, where I was stranded for several days and a couple of times nearly captured until, finally, I managed to fashion a signaling device from the elements at hand, and Va Va Voom, one of my partners in the North American Alliance for Meetness, came to my rescue in her visible plane, which is capable, thanks to the ancient technology of her homeland, Lesbo Island, of traversing interstellar distances."

And William Faulkner thought he could crank out long sentences!

The stars had now become long, varicolored lines. "How fast are we going?" I asked.

"Pretty fast," he said.

"Is the universe really curved?"

"I don't know, Will. I think you'd have to get well outside of it to be able to tell for sure. But why do you ask?"

"I was just wondering how you're able to maintain us on a straight line of travel, so that we don't waste a lot of time wandering hither and yon, or even 'curving' back toward our point of origin."

"Very astute wonderings, Will. But not to worry. My sense of Splendid Direction will keep us on an arrow-straight trajectory, at least relative to our origin-point and the universe's edge, even if there is a curvature to space that renders 'straight' objectively meaningless. We'll have to deviate now and then, naturally, so as not to collide head on with any celestial bodies, but I can intuitively nudge us right back on course."

"Glad to hear it," I said.

A speck of light suddenly appeared in the distance, oddly unaffected by the Doppler Effect, or whatever you call the thing that was making the stars look funny. "What's that?" I asked. "Off to our left, and up about thirty degrees?"

Splendid Man peered in that direction. "Well, what do you know!" he exclaimed.

"What's...?" But before I could finish my question the speck suddenly grew and resolved itself into a man. And then I recognized him. It was Northern Light, another of Splendid Man's Splendid colleagues!

"Wave, Will!"

We all waved. In less than a second, Northern Light had zoomed past us and was lost to sight.

"Wow," I said. "What do you suppose he was doing way out here?"

"Returning from the planet Eu, I imagine, to which he was no doubt summoned by the Watchdogs of the Macrocosm, those survivors of an ancient race who, with the help of a cadre of

Northern Lights, police the cosmos."

"Small universe," I said. "Ready for lunch?"

"If you are, Will," he said. "What have you got?"

"Chicken and ham," I said.

"Chicken sounds great. If you don't mind eating the ham, that is."

"Oh, no. I love ham. I also brought Fritos and a bottle of wine."

"Good thing you thought of the latter, Will," he said. "I just realized we forgot to bring a spear. When we reach the end of the universe we'll need something to throw, and the wine bottle should work nicely."

Shortly after we finished lunch the number of stars—or lines—that filled the sky started to thin out. "What's going on? " I asked. "Are we getting close to the end?"

Splendid Man was peering intently ahead. "Close to something," he said. "But not, apparently, our destination."

"Why? What do you mean?"

"You'll see in a second," he said. "Well, actually you won't really *see*. Oh, just hang on. You'll *experience* it right about…now!"

Suddenly the last star faded out and we entered a zone of absolute, stygian darkness. I'd gone spelunking deep into caves before but in comparison to this, the caves had been blindingly bright!

"Whoa," I said. "Is this what you saw? I mean, what you *didn't* see?"

"This is it."

"Do you think this is like virgin space or something, into which the universe is expanding? I mean, the universe would need space to grow into, wouldn't it?"

"I don't know, Will," Cal said. "Science has gone back and forth on the theory of an expanding universe. I can tell you one thing for sure about this zone, though. It's dark. It's very dark!"

"How's that sense of direction holding out, pal?"

"Splendidly. I wouldn't worry about that."

"Have you peered ahead with the telescopic setting of your

Splendid Vision? Any idea how long this lasts?"

"Farther than I can see," he said.

I lit a cigarette with trembling hands. No lonely traveler of the icy tundra of Earth ever derived greater comfort from a roaring fire than I did from that little glowing ember. Splendid Man asked for a smoke. I think he wanted a little spark of his own to hold onto much more than a taste of tobacco. We made small talk. I don't even remember what we talked about. We just needed to hear our voices. We made small talk and smoked cigarette after cigarette in a pathetic attempt to hold the devouring darkness at bay.

"At last!" Splendid Man exclaimed. "I see light ahead!"

"How far?" I asked.

"Why, a tad over fifteen billion light years, of course. As I explained earlier, that's as far as I can see."

"Of course," I said. "But man, that's a long time to be stuck in this darkness!"

"Not to worry. I'll put on a burst of speed and have us there in a jiffy."

By the glow of my cigarette lighter, I saw the muscles in his arms stand out. The big guy was giving it all he had!

I lost track of time. It might have been ten minutes or it might have been an hour that elapsed when even with my non-Splendid-Powered eyes I suddenly glimpsed light ahead. Then more light. Then a whole passel of light! Suddenly we were flying though a psychedelic light show unlike anything ever beheld by the eyes of man!

Well, unless they'd seen *2001, A Space Odyssey*, that is. It looked amazingly like the light show at the climax of the movie. I even found myself making Keir Dullea faces, despite the fact that I wasn't feeling any discomfort. It just seemed like the thing to do.

"Are you all right, Will?" Cal asked.

"I'm fine," I said, and made a mental note to play the movie for him sometime. "Can you see how long this goes on?"

"Not too far. No more that ten billion light years."

"Oh," I said. "That's nothing. Can you see what lies beyond?"

"Yes, I can, Will. The end of the universe itself!"

"Really? What does it look like?"

"Remember that zone of darkness we just passed through?" he said. "Well, it looks even darker than that."

"Jeepers. How can that be?"

"I don't know, Will. I'm just calling them as I see them."

Pretty soon I could feel him slackening his speed. The light show continued to play around us, but now it was easier to make out the individual whorls and curlicues or whatever shapes psychedelic phenomenon can be said to possess. Then the lights started to fade in intensity. At last, they fell behind entirely, and we came to a dead stop.

Before us, in every direction, stretched a barrier of absolute darkness. We were there. At the very end of the universe!

"Ready?" Splendid Man asked.

I passed him the empty wine bottle. "What's your guess?" I asked. "Will it bounce off or keep on going?"

"It's not going anywhere, Will. I can't determine what that barrier's composed off, but I guarantee you it's solid."

"Then why bother throwing the bottle?"

"Isn't that what we came here to do?"

He vibrated the molecules of his body through the glass of our ship and soon he was hovering outside, the bottle poised in his hand. He glanced in my direction and I gave him the thumbs up.

He reared back and hurled the bottle.

They say sound doesn't travel in space. Well, brother, whoever "they" are should have been there. The bottle hit the barrier…and the barrier shattered with a peal of thunder that must have been heard all the way back in the Richmond District!

At first I wasn't sure what I was seeing beyond the broken barrier. It was much too vast to take in at a glance. I tried craning my neck and squinting my eyes, but nothing seemed to work. And then, like with one of those puzzles you need to stare at for a long time before the intended optical effect resolves itself, I suddenly realized what it was that I beheld.

It was a face. A face of unimaginable size. A face the size of a universe. The face of a white guy with long hair and a beard. And he looked pissed. Really pissed!

I glanced at Splendid Man and for the first time in my life, and I hope the last, I saw sheer, stark terror on his face.

Then he had vibrated back into the ship and we were heading back the way we'd come, moving so fast that I thought my teeth were going to pop out the back of my head.

"Don't look back," he said. "Whatever you do, don't look back!"

"Who do you think I am?" I said. "Orpheus? Ain't no way I'm looking back, brother!"

•••

We'd sent out for pizza and we sat in my dining room eating our fill and guzzling beer. "So what do you think?" I asked. "Was that God we saw?"

Cal thought about that for a minute. "I find that hard to believe," he finally said. "Back on Strontium we had many different faiths, but whether we worshipped Jeez'In, Yahw'In, All'In, or Brahm'In, we believed in a God of love. This…entity we saw seemed anything *but* loving. He looked about as angry as anybody I've ever seen, even Giganto the Splendid Mandrill when I trapped him in the distant past."

"Let's not forget that we broke his window," I said.

"There's that," he admitted. "But still."

"What if he was some Splendid Being?" I postulated. "One that dwarfs you in power the way you dwarf us mere humans?"

Cal shook his head. "I suspect we'll never know, Will. I, for one, have no intention of returning to the ends of the universe. And if I ever should find myself in the vicinity, I sure won't throw anything at the barrier again."

"Perhaps we learned a lesson today," I said. "That, this side of the grave, there are secrets no man may ever know."

"Perhaps you're right, Will. And more, secrets that no man may ever presume to unravel."

"Like, did the universe have a creator?"

"And do all beings possess immortal souls?"
"And is Va Va Voom really a lesbian?"
We speculated deep into the night.

Made in the USA
San Bernardino, CA
15 October 2015